# Love Speaks

## *An Everlasting Love*

### BY
### DAVID CARR

D1416012

ISBN: 9798667148845 (paperback)

# DEDICATION

I would like to dedicate this book to my many friends that were always by our side during thick and thin, to my loving and faith filled family, and to my amazing wife, Marianela. Above all, I dedicate this book to my God who gave me the time, the encouragement and the words. Thank you for the miracles in our lives.

# CONTENTS

# INTRODUCTION

Recently I attended Sunday Mass, and the priest said he believed each one of us had a mission to accomplish on this earth. This statement got me to reflect on my life. I believe that our given mission can only be completed by each of us. I also believe that God gives us the ability to accomplish it. I believe that my mission is to tell my story to honor God.

I retired in 2012, ending a forty-seven-year engineering career in television broadcasting. During those years, I was a part of converting television facilities from black and white to color, from monaural to stereo, from analog to digital, and, finally, from standard definition to high definition. I always considered myself very lucky to have been given these opportunities. I also managed two renovation projects that involved not only building modifications but also technical ones. As a result of this, I became well known in the broadcasting field, and I was often featured in many trade magazines.

While all those years in broadcasting gave me much satisfaction, I realized that there had to be something else to life. I knew God had to somehow have another mission for me. Surely I wasn't put on this earth to build television facilities. This came to light when I realized that, shortly after I retired,

my hard work quickly faded away. Television, like other tech-
nologies, was ever evolving. Past accomplishments were soon
replaced and forgotten—although the lower rungs of a ladder
were just as necessary to support the upper ones.

Surely there had to be more to life than this. But what?

# 1

# MY CHILDHOOD

Since the beginning, my childhood was somewhat unique. I was born in Laredo, Texas, in 1946. That was not the unique part. The special element was that I am an identical twin.

Medical science in 1946 was not what it is today. In 1946, a pregnant mother was x-rayed only occasionally for fear of overexposure to the radiation. Sonograms did not exist. As a result, it wasn't until a week before my arrival that the doctor x-rayed my mother and surprised my parents with the news that there were two of us. Dad used to tell us that, up until that time, he thought he had already purchased all the baby furniture and other items needed, only to find out that he was half done.

My father came from a small family with only his mother and a half sister, who died early in his life. My mother, however, came from a large family. She had one sister and six brothers. They all lived with my grandparents in a house that my grandfather and his sons built. When my grandfather bought the property, it comprised a ditch, so he used that to construct a basement for the house. He had to fill the ditch anyway, so he might as well fill it with usable space. Not too many houses in South Texas had basements, but this one did.

My grandfather died just before my father and mother got married. My mother persuaded my father to live in that house so that my grandmother would not be alone. All her siblings had already left, most of them to serve in the military.

My twin brother, Dan, and I lived in that house with my parents and grandmother until about age twenty. Those years were very memorable. My grandmother often had friends come to visit, to chat and enjoy a cup of coffee. Whenever they dropped in, my brother and I were sent to the corner bakery to buy sweet bread so that she could enjoy it with her friends. As soon as we arrived with the bread, we would get a glance from my mother or grandmother, indicating that we should leave the room and let the adults talk. One time we were given a one-dollar bill and asked to go to the bakery. My brother was absolutely certain that my grandmother told him to buy the whole dollar's worth of crescents. The lady at the bakery asked him if he was sure that he was supposed to buy a whole dollar's worth. He was definite. The lady cleared the entire counter and had to go to the back to complete the order. We walked back home, both of us carrying a large bag full of bread. My grandmother was surprised to see that much bread. She told us that she only wanted twenty-five cents' worth. We walked back and returned most of the bread. For the many years that followed, my brother insisted that my grandmother had asked for one dollar's worth of bread. He never admitted that he was wrong. Since Dan was the one carrying the dollar, I said I had nothing to do with it.

Whenever my brother and I would do something wrong, my mother said, "Go to the basement and wait until your father gets home. He'll take care of you." This was her way of getting us out of her hair. This later gave way to the now well-known time-out. We spent so much time down in the basement that we decided it would be a good plan to keep our toys down there.

My mother was a very nervous person and scared of new kitchen knives that were given to her. I remember her telling us not to touch them; being new, they were too sharp to use. She would always put the sets of knives in the basement for safekeeping. These became great toys for my brother and me to play with. One time we found a huge box of wool that my grandmother stored down in the basement. Her intention was to sew a quilt with her friends using that wool. Since it had been there for some time, the box of wool became the perfect target for us to throw the knives into. We did this so much that two things happened. First, we got very good at it. Second, one side of the box completely disintegrated due to our knife throws. We had to turn that side toward the wall so my mother would not see it whenever she went into the basement. When the day finally arrived to quilt, my grandmother and her friends were shocked to see a three-sided box. My brother and I tried to convince my mom that we had rats…yeah, and their names were Dan and David.

My brother and I attended St. Augustine School. That school was a three-story building located next to St. Augustine

Church. The school went from first to twelfth grade. This parochial school offered a very spiritual education. All but one grade had nuns as teachers. St. Augustine Church was where my brother and I received baptism, reconciliation, communion, and confirmation. It was also where my wife and I were married many years later.

After our First Holy Communion, the photographer was there to take the group picture in front of the church. When we all lined up for the picture, my brother noticed that the boy next to him had his candle right in front of his face. To improve the picture, my brother reached over and lowered the boy's hands. The boy moved them back up. This happened about three times before the two of them started throwing punches. I guess that the spirit of Holy Communion had not taken effect on either one of them yet.

When we were about ten years old, my brother and I were enrolled in piano lessons at school. Sister Helen Agnes was our music teacher. We didn't particularly care for the daily practice, and, most of all, we disliked having to play in a recital in front of family and friends. Being twins created a special challenge for us. Our teacher thought it would be a good idea to have each of us play one song separately, followed by a song that we would play together. The night of the recital, my brother went on stage and played his song. He made his exit. I then came onto the stage. The audience laughed, thinking Dan forgot that he had another song to play. I finished my song and exited. Next, we both walked on stage and played our duet. At that point, the audience realized there were two of us.

Although they were not wealthy, our parents managed to educate us in a Catholic school, from kindergarten through high school. My brother and I attended kindergarten and first grade at Mary Help of Christians. After first grade, Mary Help of Christians became an all-girls school, so we had to transfer to St. Augustine. It seemed that we flunked the physical!

The school was next door to the church, so we went to 8:00 a.m. Mass Monday through Friday prior to starting our classes. On the Thursday before every first Friday of the month, we were paraded into church by the nuns so that we could go to confession. This, of course, was to prepare us to receive Holy Communion on the first Friday. I recall going to confession one summer evening, only to be asked by the priest, sitting behind the little screen, why I hadn't gone to confession that afternoon with the other children. I, very innocently, replied that it was because I didn't have a ride. He asked me very abruptly if I didn't have any legs. At this point, I remembered that this priest had his legs amputated and had been confined to a wheelchair for many years. I didn't answer; I simply got up and left before he added more to my penance.

The other ritual that we observed at that time was to abstain from eating meat on Fridays. The only exception, according to some, was if you were in Mexico. This was because of the poverty in Mexico. The logic was to allow people to eat meat whenever it was available to them. So some people from the US would simply go across the river into Nuevo Laredo, have awesome feasts, come back, and tell us all about it. Since my parents rarely went to Nuevo Laredo, the chances of us being there on a Friday were slim to none. This just didn't seem fair.

My mother was overprotective, and firmly believed that my brother and I could do no wrong. When we were in third grade, the boys in the class seemed to divide into two groups of friends. While this seemed innocent at first, it later grew into two sides that often turned into confrontations. Most of them took place at recess. We thought that the teacher was not aware of it. When my mother went to the school office to register us for fourth grade, she noticed that our files had the remark *always fighting*. She asked the office attendant if that meant that we were always fighting to get good grades. The lady laughed and clarified the statement. My mother was not happy when she got home. Yes, we went back to the basement.

My mother always dressed my brother and me alike. Being identical and dressing similarly made it easy for us to play pranks on our teachers and schoolmates. Every year we would have school pictures taken. Once the pictures were developed, the teacher would always call out the student's name so that the pictures could be given to each child. In our case, the nun would just say, "Carr," and hand out both packets together so we could decide which ones belonged to whom.

Playing pranks on our teachers was fun. Since my brother and I were identical twins, and since we used to dress alike all the time, our teachers often had trouble telling us apart. Whenever one of us did something wrong, we would always point to the other one as being the culprit. This would some-times get us out of the punishment, but more often than not, it would frustrate the nuns—thus escalating the results.

Although I can recall the names of all my teachers, one es-pecially stood out: Sister Goretti. She was the math and science teacher, and she was tough. Her homeroom was in ninth grade. Her reputation preceded her. When I was in eighth grade, she would come into our room to teach us advanced math. We all dreaded that period. But more than that, we worried about the next year when she would be our homeroom teacher. But somehow we all made it through her algebra and trigonometry classes. We finally were able to breathe a sigh of relief when we finished ninth grade. We had a great summer vacation, knowing the worst was behind us. However, when we showed up on the first day of tenth grade, our jaws dropped. Yes, there she was, sitting in the chair reserved for the homeroom teacher. She had been reassigned to tenth grade. We had just been had.

I became a very good student in math and science, mostly because I was afraid of her. I recall winning an award for a science experiment. I wanted to prove that low air pressure affected the complete blood count (CBC). To verify this, I special ordered two white mice. My mother wasn't too happy when they showed up. And, yes, again she sent me to the basement.

The basement was now my lab, and my problem was how to get a CBC for two white mice. I called the nun in charge of the lab at Mercy Hospital. She was nice enough to take blood samples from each mouse. The first sample was taken at the beginning of the experiment. The CBC of each mouse was similar. I had two bell jars, one for each mouse. After placing a mouse in each bell jar, I sealed each jar with wax at the bottom. I kept one at normal air pressure, and I lowered the air pressure of the other with the use of an aerator. I connected this device to the top of the bell jar and a water faucet. Whenever I ran water through the device, it vacuumed air out of the bell jar. Two weeks later I took the mice back for another blood test, and the results verified my hypothesis. The mouse under normal pressure showed no change. The mouse under low air pressure had a significant increase in red blood cells. The lower air pressure meant a lower oxygen content, so the red blood cells increased to compensate for the reduction in oxygen.

My mother was glad that I received an award, but she was happier to know that I was able to sell the mice and no longer kept them in the basement.

Dan and I were blessed with parents who came from very religious families. Their faith was very strong, and for that, I am grateful. Our parents would pass on their faith on to us all. Fortunately, Marianela's parents did the same for her. This prepared us for our married life together, and we both focused on passing this faith on to our family.

# 2

# THE DATING YEARS

During my high school years, I belonged to the school and church choirs. I think I first joined the choir just to get out of class. But as it turned out, the choir would later play a very important part in my life. Members of the church choir included a few young boys and girls, but it was mostly older ladies. There were two ladies in particular who I used to refer to as *the clowns*, given the amount of makeup they applied. Their loud singing wasn't too appealing to me either.

In August 1961, Father Henry Janssen, the choir director, decided to take the choir on a picnic. A seminarian whose family owned a lot on Lake Casa Blanca made his property available to us. This event was called a *lunada*. In Spanish, it means "a feast under the light of the moon." Little did I know that night would change my life forever. While others grilled burgers and hot dogs, I was under a spell cast on me by a beautiful young girl. I had never seen her before, but I could not take my eyes off her. I knew I needed to meet her and get to know her, but there were so many people around her, and I was just too shy to talk to her. I was satisfied to discover her name: Marianela. Such a beautiful name for such a beautiful girl. The evening ended, and I still had not spoken to her. She probably didn't know I was there.

I immediately began doing my homework to get to know her. I can't recall how I found out, but I quickly discovered her phone number and where she lived. I knew I had to call her. I had to let her know I existed. But what if she didn't care for me? Maybe she will once she gets to know me. I just had to take the chance. I couldn't lose her.

Somehow I was able to muster enough courage to make that first call. When I heard her voice, I was speechless. But I had to say something before she hung up. I told her my name and that I had seen her at the *lunada* but hadn't had the opportunity to talk to her. I couldn't tell her I just didn't have the nerve to do it. Suddenly it dawned on me how I could distinguish myself from all the other boys there. I told her that I was one of the twins.

She said, "Oh yes, I remember because I met your brother." At least she talked to my stand-in. Since my twin and I were alike, maybe it was really like talking to me…sort of. Anyway, this got my foot in the door and got me recognized.

Marianela, at that time, attended Mary Help of Christians, the all-girls school that I had attended many years earlier. On the one hand, I didn't get to see her every day, but on the other hand, I was glad she didn't have any boys in her class who I would have to compete with.

The St. Augustine School festival had been scheduled for October. I thought this would be the perfect opportunity to ask her out. I was extremely nervous, but I forced myself to call to ask her if she wanted to attend the festival with me. To my surprise, she accepted. I then asked if she wanted me to drive over to pick her up. She said her parents would bring her to the festival. This was good and bad news. The bad news was that I couldn't pick her up, and the good news was that she came from a very loving, protective family.

Some weeks prior to the festival, the tenth-grade students were told that our grade was to have the doll booth. With the use of a roulette wheel, our booth would make money by giving away beautifully dressed dolls. People would buy numbers and wait to see if their number came up on the roulette wheel. If it did, they would select one of the dolls. Where did the dolls come from? Well, weeks before the festival, the nuns gave each student a doll to take home. Unfortunately, all the dolls were naked. How embarrassing! I took my naked doll home, hiding it in my book satchel so no one would see me with it. My mother took it to a seamstress to get an outfit. I was just glad that I didn't have to look at that naked doll anymore.

On the day of the festival, many of the parents went to the schoolyard to help set up all the booths. I went with my parents to help as well. While there, Sister Goretti came up to me and asked me if I had my doll with me. I told her that I did not but that *she* would be joining me later that evening. As bright as she was, the sister failed to see the humor in that statement, and I didn't understand why.

Another thing happened the morning of the festival. I had a close encounter of the dangerous kind. A guy who I had never met before came up to me and told me not to take Marianela to the festival. If I did, he would have no option but to beat me up. Hmm, now what? I mentioned that to my brother, Dan, and he said not to worry about it. Well, I did worry about it but decided that if I was going to get beaten up, Marianela was well worth it. The night of the festival, I met up with this beautiful girl. I quickly noticed that my brother and a friend of his were behind us. His friend used to be a body-builder. I felt so proud to be walking around the festival with her. It wasn't until years later that Marianela understood why my brother never left our side the entire evening. Dan had my back. Oh, I never saw the other guy again.

At the time, Marianela was thirteen years old, and I was fifteen. She was starting eighth grade, and I was starting tenth grade. Since Mary Help of Christians School only went up to eighth grade, she transferred to St. Augustine School the following year. Now I could see her every day. I looked forward to lunchtime when I could talk to her for about ten minutes. After school, I would walk her home and carry her books. So what if the temperature got to 105 degrees? What mattered was that I was with her.

St. Augustine High School had a very limited sports program, mostly due to the lack of space at the facility. The sport of choice was basketball. Marianela and I attended every home game. Her parents would drop her off at the gym and pick her up at the end of the game. Although I was already driving, having her ride in my car was completely out of the question. Those were very innocent years, and I was fine with that.

One time, Marianela told her girlfriend that she could tell me apart from my brother. Although everyone thought we were identical, Marianela told her friend that she knew us well enough to distinguish one from the other. One night, she and her girlfriend walked into the gym. Her friend went in another direction but kept looking back while Marianela walked up to my brother. Dan pointed over to me, indicating that he was not the one she was looking for. Her friend just nodded her head and laughed. Perhaps it would take more time before she would be able to tell us apart.

It seemed that, in those days, we could not spend enough time together. We would go to the movies, which, by the way, cost me fifty cents for each of us, plus twenty-five cents more for two hot dogs. What can I say? I was a big spender. Of course, her younger sister would always accompany us. This was a requirement imposed by parents. I later realized how many movies we had seen when the Academy Awards aired, and I was familiar with all the movies nominated.

Marianela and I would also go to all the church bingos. I soon had the bingo schedule of all the churches in Laredo. I don't recall ever winning any bingo games, but I do recall feeling very fortunate to be with my girl.

Marianela gave me a beautiful dark green sweater one Christmas. When I took it home to show my parents, my mother asked where she had purchased it. I told her that I didn't know but would ask her. I knew where this was going. How could I have a sweater and my brother not have an identical one? That couldn't be. Once I found out where Marianela had purchased it, I told my mother. She went to the store only to be told that my sweater was the last one they had. You would think that's where this would end. But no, of course it wasn't. My mother thought it perfectly logical to take my sweater, the one that Marianela had personally selected, and exchange it for one that the store had two of. To say that this didn't sit well with Marianela would be an understatement.

We continued to date and attended school dances. Like always, her parents would drop her off at the school and then pick her up at the appointed time. One time while we were dancing, I happened to look out a window of the gym, and I saw her mother standing outside looking at me. Seriously?

Years later Marianela told me that her parents had agreed to allow me to pick her up at her house. I had finally built up enough credibility with them. They trusted me. As I drove away with Marianela, I noticed her parents driving behind us. They followed us all the way to our destination. I thought they trusted me, but now that I am a father of three daughters, I completely understand.

When Marianela turned fifteen, she, like all the other Hispanic girls, was given a *quinceañera* party. This special birthday party is celebrated as the girl is presented as a young lady into society. Up until this time, she had been a girl. The young lady invites fourteen of her closest friends to be her *damas*. Each one represents the previous fourteen years of her life. All fifteen girls have escorts. Each couple is introduced as they enter the hall, and they line up on either side, leaving the center for the honoree and her date. At this time, the first dance takes place between the honoree and her escort. I still remember that waltz. The song was called "Fascination," and that moment certainly was fascinating. The second dance is reserved for the father of the young lady. Most of the time, the parents of all the girls and their escorts are in attendance. Other friends and family members also attend. As you can see, this is a rather elaborate gathering—one that often seems like a wedding reception. I was honored to be Marianela's escort that night.

I was also her escort at the quinceañera parties for all of her friends. Those were indeed beautiful and memorable years. My poor parents spent so much money on countless wrist corsages.

Heavenly Father, thank you for this absolutely beautiful courtship. I know that all these years were a precursor to many more years that we had together.

Marianela, I am so happy that together we looked forward to making all our dreams come true.

# 3

# THE WEDDING

As the years passed, Marianela and I began planning our wedding. I was at the University of Texas in Austin, and she was still in high school. We both got part-time jobs to start saving money for our wedding and future together. We bought a living room, dining room, and bedroom furniture set, along with a stove and refrigerator, using a layaway plan. I also bought the engagement ring. We did this without our parents' knowledge.

On Christmas Eve 1965, I went to pick up Marianela at her house and bring her to my house to wish my parents and grandmother a merry Christmas. We exchanged gifts. My Christmas gift for her was a thirty-five-millimeter camera. Yes, it used film. We then left my house and headed to hers. I stopped the car along the way. When I turned toward her, she asked what was wrong.

I said, "Nothing is wrong."

It was then that I proposed to her. Once she said yes, I placed the ring on her finger. I never stopped thanking her for allowing me to be part of her life.

Once we got to her house, she showed her parents, sister, and grandmother the ring and told them that I had proposed and that she had accepted. Everyone was so happy. We exchanged gifts there as well. I also took pictures with Marianela's new camera. When the evening was over, I left to go back to my house. While I was driving home, Marianela's mother called my mother to thank her for wanting to have their daughter in our family. She also told her that the ring was beautiful. My mother politely said it was their pleasure and ended the conversation.

After I got home, my mother greeted me at the door with fire in her eyes. She wanted to know why she had not been made aware that I was going to propose and already purchased the ring. Did I mention that my mother was a very controlling Hispanic mother?

Nothing could take away the glow from my face or the specialness of that evening. I told her that both she and Dad knew that we would eventually be married. We had been dating since that festival in 1961. I was just glad that the cat was out of the bag and, most of all, that Marianela and I were beginning the next phase of our lives.

When we were engaged, Marianela was a senior in high school and had just turned eighteen. I was still at the University of Texas and was twenty. Looking back at that, I can understand how concerned my parents were. But now I see that the hand of God was with us, leading us every step of the way and keeping us safe.

In the days prior to our wedding, all of my friends would always ask me the same question.

"Are you nervous?"

I would reflect on this and would answer that I did not feel nervous at all. This was true until the wedding got closer. Actually, as I stepped into the sacristy of the church before the wedding, my knees began shaking. I could not stop them from shaking, no matter what I tried.

Somehow I was able to walk through the sacristy out to the altar. My brother and best man, Dan, and I stood at the front of the church as the bridesmaids and maid of honor slowly walked up the aisle and lined up in front of the first pew. Now everything was quiet. After a short pause, the music began to play again. I looked down the aisle and saw the most beautiful sight that I have ever seen. There she was standing next to her father, but I don't recall seeing him at all. I just saw her slowly walking up the aisle and over the lovely rose petals that the flower girl had dropped. With every step that she took, my heart beat faster. *Is this really happening? Is she actually walking to me to start a new life together?* I realized that my knees were no longer shaking. I felt so safe with her by my side. This secure feeling stayed with me for the rest of our married life because she was always with me, supporting me, reassuring me, and encouraging me in whatever life brought us.

*A woman's beauty makes her husband's face light up, for it surpasses all else that charms the eye. A wife is her husband's richest treasure, a helpmate, a steadying column.*
*—Sirach 36:22, 24 (New American Bible Version)*

My Lord, how grateful I am to you for the priceless gift you have given me today.

# 4

# OUR SON

On June 10, 1967, my beautiful Marianela and I were married in St. Augustine Church. In 1968, we had our first daughter, also named Marianela. We called her Mari. My wife was called Nelly to distinguish them from each other. Two years later we had our second daughter, Anjanette, and our third daughter, Roxanne, was born in 1974. Our daughters are all very special and precious to my wife and me.

On November 8, 1978, our Lord blessed us with a son, David Jr. As a sidenote, all of our children were born by cesarean section. Our son was a few weeks premature, so he was taken to a hospital that specialized in neonatal care. By the time my wife woke up from the anesthesia, our son had already been transported to the other hospital. She was so eager to see him. She kept asking me to describe him to her.

I tried my best but could only come up with, "He's the best-looking baby there."

In those few days, I went back and forth from one hospital to the other. Tickling our son's little feet was truly awesome. I went out and bought a Polaroid camera and took pictures of our son so that Marianela could see him. My wife and I would just hold each other and stare at the pictures, waiting for the day we would all be home. Some very close friends of ours brought us a bottle of champagne to celebrate that we now had a son. Once again, life couldn't be better.

> *So he went to him and kissed him. When Isaac caught the smell of his clothes, he blessed him and said, "Ah, the smell of my son is like the smell of a field that the Lord has blessed."*
> —*Genesis 27:27(New American Bible Version)*

One evening my wife and I received a call from the pediatrician. He told us that our son was doing so well that they had been able to take him off the ventilator. This meant that we would soon be home together as a family. Later that evening after visiting hours were over, I went home to check up on our daughters. They were being looked after by a very good friend of ours. She was actually the wife of the pediatrician. I remember pulling up into the driveway and her running out to me.

With tears in her eyes, she said, "Go back to the hospital. There's something wrong with your baby."

I saw my girls standing at the door with a confused look. I reassured them that all would be fine. I rushed back, praying during the entire drive, feeling just as confused as my daughters were. When I arrived at the hospital, I was told that somehow my baby had contracted sepsis, an infection in his blood; the only way he might be saved would be to have all his blood replaced. I agreed to donate my blood so that this could be done. As the doctor prepared to start the procedure, I got some water and baptized my baby boy. I stood there as the neonatologist removed a small amount of his blood and added some of mine. This procedure seemed to take forever. I prayed the entire time and asked God to save our son. I bargained with God to the best of my ability. But it was not to be; God had other plans.

*The Lord came and stood there, calling as at the other times, "Samuel! Samuel!" Then Samuel said, "Speak, for your servant is listening."*
                                    —*1 Samuel 3:10 (New American Bible Version)*

Forty-four hours into his life, David Jr. went to be with our Lord. I was in total disbelief. *Why?* Was it because of my sins that my son had to pay with his life?

As I drove to the other hospital, I prayed and asked God for the right words to tell Marianela. How would I be able to break the news to her? But then, when I opened the door to her hospital room, no words were necessary. We just simply held each other and wept. The pain in my heart was unbearable, but I was certain that it couldn't come close to what she was feeling. She never got to see him. She never got to hold him.

And she made a vow, saying,

*O Lord Almighty, if you will only look upon your servant's misery and remember me, and not forget your servant but give*

*her a son, then I will give him to the Lord for all the days of his life, and no razor will ever be used on his head.*
        —*1 Samuel 1:11 (New American Bible Version)*

Afterward I had to go home and tell his older sisters. With tears in my eyes, I held them and told them that we now had an angel in heaven looking out after us. All three girls stood around me, crying, with confused looks. We held each other as they asked why this had to happen. None of us had an answer.

They simply said, "Life is not fair." I could only agree.

*Now Israel's eyes were failing because of old age, and he could hardly see. So Joseph brought his children close to him, and his father kissed them and embraced them.*
        —*Genesis 48:10 (New American Bible Version)*

God, how could you do this to us? You had us on such a high and then slammed us as low and hard as you could. Why did you do this? We have always been faithful to you and worked for you. What did we do wrong? We don't deserve this.

Marianela kept telling me that she felt so hurt, and she no longer wanted to have anything to do with God. We still went to Mass, but it now seemed cold and distant. We no longer felt the passion to do his work. We had been working with Marriage Encounter, a marriage enrichment movement in the Catholic Church, prior to this event. We decided to stop this apostolate. We didn't believe we had anything to share with others. We certainly could no longer share God's love, because it seemed we no longer felt God's love.

The pediatrician and his wife were very close friends of ours. They were like our brother and sister. They were also active in Marriage Encounter. Sometime later they invited us—no, they actually almost dragged us—to a Reconciliation Weekend put on by Marriage Encounter. It was during this weekend that we began to feel God's peace. We realized that we had to forgive God in order for our lives to begin growing spiritually once again. With each passing day, my wife, daughters, and I gradually rebuilt our lives. We began to realize that our Lord had not left us. It was us that had left him. He had been there all along, patiently waiting for us to be ready to open our hearts and let him back in. Attending church had meaning to us once more. It was like coming home.

*"Father, I have sinned against heaven and against You; I no longer deserve to be called your son." But the father said to his servants, "Quick! Bring the best robe and put it on him. Put a ring on his finger and sandals on his feet. Then let us celebrate with a feast, because this son of mine was dead, and has come to life again; he was lost and has been found." Then the celebration began.*

—*Luke 15:21–24 (New American Bible Version)*

Two of our daughters have married two wonderful, caring men, and each has three children. Our oldest daughter, Mari, married Raul, and they have three girls: Analiese, Roxanne, and Lauren. Our youngest daughter, Roxanne, married Nathan, and they have a son and two daughters: David, Kaylie, and Meredith. All three daughters made a pact after our son went to be with our Lord. They agreed that whoever would have the first boy would name him David. I did not know this until after my grandson David's birth.

Life isn't fair, but it's good—at least for a while. But as we all know, life has its ups and downs.

Dear Lord, I know that you also lost your son. May I have the faith necessary to also accept the loss of my son. I also ask the Blessed Mother to help Marianela as she copes with the loss of our son.

# 5

## GOD'S PRESENCE

The passing of our son was truly challenging for all of us. I don't think I will ever understand why this happened. All I know is that, during this and other trying times in our lives, we have always felt our Lord's presence. His love was manifested by the many members of our support community. We have lived in Laredo, San Antonio, Houston, Phoenix, and Dallas. In all these places, our family has always felt God's love, especially during difficult times.

Just as Marianela and I made it a point to always be there for our family, we have always had our spiritual family by our side. I have always heard that we are the body of Christ. We are his hands and feet. I have now seen Christ's body at work in our lives.

When we lost our son, we had friends reaching out to us from across the country and even from Mexico City. Often, they would call us to ask what they could do to help and to reassure us that they were praying for us. This support helped Marianela and me to be there for our daughters and for each other. This time in our lives was difficult. If we as adults didn't understand the loss of our son, how could our daughters? As time passed, we all were there for each other.

I still recall bringing Marianela home from the hospital. I had already disassembled the crib that I had prepared for our son's arrival. How difficult it was, seeing Marianela on the floor, folding all the baby clothes and blankets that would never be used by our son. One by one she looked at them, folded them, and placed them in her cedar chest, which served as her hope chest years earlier.

Even through our pain, we needed to be there for our daughters, who were also mourning the loss of their brother. It is in times like these, when our inner pain is so strong, that we must be there for the others who are also grieving.

During the next few years, we lost other family members. One day, in 1983, my mother called my father from work, trying to coordinate their work schedules in order to synchronize days for their vacation. Hours after her call, my father received a call from one of my mom's coworkers. He was informed that my mother had suddenly complained of a severe headache. Seconds later she collapsed on the floor. An ambulance took her to the local hospital, and examinations revealed that she had suffered an aneurysm. By then, my father was already at the hospital. He was told that they would be transferring her from the hospital in Laredo to one in San Antonio. Unfortunately, she passed while in transit.

Ten years later my father passed from complications of diabetes. He had been dealing with diabetes for many years.

This disease had claimed his eyesight, kidneys, and both legs. Marianela and I visited him with our daughters. He would use his hands to touch their faces and imagine what the girls looked like.

My brother and I were very close. One day he called me and asked what I was doing. I told him that I had ridden a roller coaster three consecutive times. He asked me to stop because he had a very bad headache, which he attributed to me riding those rides.

On a separate occasion, I woke up in the early hours of the morning in extreme pain. Marianela took me to the hospital, and I was diagnosed as having a kidney stone. Later that morning Marianela called my brother. His wife answered the phone and told her that my brother had not slept all night due to a severe pain. When I finally passed the stone, the pain left both of us.

Years later Marianela and I were vacationing on a beach. Suddenly I felt a chest pain. She saw my reaction and became concerned. I told her that I had a chest pain but that she shouldn't worry; I thought I was not the one having the problem. I called my brother and was informed that he had just had a heart attack.

On another occasion, his wife called me and asked if I was having another kidney stone. I told her that I was fine.

She said, "I guess this one is his."

It was.

My twin brother, Dan, also passed from diabetes complications in 2010. He lost his kidneys and his eyesight. The weekend prior to his passing, Marianela, our daughters, and I visited him in a hospital in Corpus Christi. His condition was grave. We spent some time with him and tried to cheer him up. We noticed that he was having trouble accepting his condition. It appeared that he was afraid of dying. Marianela leaned over and began speaking softly to him, reassuring him that all would be in God's hands and that he should accept God's will.

Suddenly, he raised his head, stared at her, and shouted, "No!"

We realized that he needed prayers. We prayed for him, wished him well, and said goodbye before heading back to San Antonio.

Days later I called and said farewell to him, knowing that I would never see him again. The next day while I was in my office, I suddenly had a very strong sensation that he had just passed. I saw myself in his room. There he was, lying lifeless in his bed. Minutes later I received a call from his son notifying me of his passing.

As previously mentioned, Dan and I often played pranks on others. The last time that we did this was rather inadvertently. My family and I went to his funeral service. He had been cremated, so his picture was next to his remains at the front of the church. It was a very somber event—that is, until the priest noticed me. He briefly paused, looked at Dan's picture, then looked at me. He did this several times. Then he realized that he had to continue speaking. His facial expression spoke volumes. It was apparent that he was not aware that Dan and I were twins. I'm certain that Dan got a good laugh, as did I.

Dan and I always had a very close relationship. Our bond as twins often allowed us to have entire conversations without uttering a single word. We could be across the room and know what the other was thinking by just a glance. Days after his passing, we conversed again. I saw him next to me as if he were still alive.

He smiled and simply said, "Nothing to it." No other conversation was needed.

Marianela and I continued praying with and for our daughters, asking God to see us through these episodes in our lives. We have always been blessed with a reassurance that God is with us in both our joy and sorrow.

Dear God, although I feel tremendous pain in my heart for the loss of my son and other family members, I see others in my family mourning as well. I ask that you continue to be with us, healing us with your love. Amen.

# 6

# SUMMERTIME

When our grandchildren were young, Marianela began a beautiful tradition. She called it Lita Camp. As a sidenote, our grandchildren call me Papa David and call Marianela Lita, which is short for *abuelita* (grandmother in Spanish). Every summer, she would create an invitation for this event. It would list the places to be visited and the fun projects to be enjoyed, and, at the end, it would read: "depending on good behavior." Our grandchildren would look forward to this two-week vacation every year. Upon arrival, each child would get a welcome letter and a schedule of events. Since we lived in San Antonio, Houston, Phoenix, and Dallas, the locations and projects would vary.

San Antonio would allow us to visit The Alamo, the Witte Museum, Brackenridge Park, the San Antonio Zoo, Fiesta Texas, SeaWorld, and the River Walk. Sometimes we would even go to other missions besides The Alamo.

In Houston, we went to AstroWorld, the Astrodome for a baseball game, various museums, and the Battleship Texas in the San Jacinto battlegrounds. Nearby Galveston, Texas, meant we spent a day at the beach, enjoyed excellent seafood, and planned a side trip to NASA.

The Heard Museum in Phoenix provided fun education for both our grandchildren and us. Given the hot days in Phoenix, we would always have a day in the pool. Short trips around the area included Scottsdale, the beautiful red rock formations of Sedona, Flagstaff, and, of course, the Grand Canyon. Sometimes we would go to the small town of Holbrook, Arizona. This trip would take us along the famous Route 66.

In Dallas, we visited the Dallas Museum of Art, Six Flags in Arlington, the Texas School Book Depository, the Dallas Arboretum, the Dallas World Aquarium, the Dallas Zoo, and Galleria Dallas for some ice-skating and shopping. We also attended Texas Rangers baseball games.

During each Lita Camp, my wife would take plenty of pictures and give each family a photo album to commemorate the visit at the end. Each child would also get a personalized certificate of completion. All my grandchildren often recall the various Lita Camps and the fun they had. Above all, they recall how special Lita made it for them.

Another tradition that Marianela started was taking each grandchild on a vacation when they turned twelve years old. This allowed them to enjoy special time with just us without their siblings. We allowed each of them to select the location for their trip.

Analiese chose to go to San Juan, Puerto Rico, for her vacation. Once there, we visited El Yunque National Forest, which is the only tropical rain forest in the United States National Forest System. This half day excursion took us up to the Sierra de Luquillo Mountains to experience all the vegetation and examine closely numerous classes of flowers. The next day we toured the Bacardi distillery and learned the Bacardi history, including why there is a bat on every bottle of rum produced. It is considered a symbol of good luck. The adults also got to sample their products. In Old San Juan, we toured El Morro, which is an old fort that defended the island against invaders centuries ago. This location was selected because it provided a good view of any ships wanting to invade them. Old San Juan also provided a perfect opportunity for us to conquer the stores. Beautiful clothes, handbags, and souvenirs were the order of the day.

Roxanne (Sanny) asked to go to Vancouver, Canada. Unfortunately, I was not able to accompany Sanny and Marianela on this trip. My work schedule would not allow it. This is the only trip that I missed. Marianela and Sanny flew into Seattle and took a bus to Vancouver. They were met by two friends of ours who lived in The Woodlands, Texas, just north of Houston. They actually lived in The Woodlands during the winter months and in Vancouver in the summer.

Here are the events as recalled by Roxanne.

That was a fun trip. When we first got there, we found out the airline had lost my luggage, so we had to get that straightened out. Then as we were walking to Anna's car, Lita fell in a bush. She didn't scream or make any noise, which was surprising. We were walking side by side, and suddenly she was gone! We were laughing so hard after I helped her up. When we arrived at Anna's house, she gave us a tour of the house and showed us two pans that she had behind the dresser. She said that those were for the bears. I thought she was kidding—until there was an actual bear in the backyard. I screamed for Lita. Lita screamed for Anna. Anna came into the room and started banging the two pans to shoo the bear away. The next morning Anna made some *arroz con leche* for breakfast. It was the best rice pudding I had ever had. Actually, I think it was the first one I had ever had. Later we went to Chinatown. The people there were very friendly. We watched them make fortune cookies. I also got to buy some delicious maple syrup and enjoy some very tasty fish and chips. On another occasion, we took a ferry to the house of Anna's friends. They told us they were going to serve us salmon. Lita leaned over to me and whispered that the fish might have some bones. I remember being terrified as to what kind of dinner I had walked into. The dinner ended up being very good. Overall, it was a really fun trip, and I am still so grateful to have been given the opportunity to travel with Lita.

Lauren selected San Francisco as her destination. Once there we visited the Ghirardelli Square, Fisherman's Wharf, Chinatown, and Little Italy, which satisfied our appetites. We also went down Lombard Street, to the Golden Gate Bridge, and took a ferry to Alcatraz. On another day, we drove to the wine country and toured various wineries in Napa Valley and Sonoma. Of course, a trip to San Francisco would not be complete without a trolley ride. Lauren kept asking her grandmother if she could ride the trolley while hanging out the side. She asked so many times that we finally gave in. When Lauren stood up, held on to the pole, and leaned out, Lita hung on to Lauren by her blouse. We still laugh whenever we recall that scene. I remember being often winded while going up and down those hills. Lita and I were always lagging behind Lauren. She would walk ahead and then wait at the next intersection for us to catch up.

When we asked Dave where he wanted to go, he said he just wanted to see a volcano. After some research, I determined that there was one in northeastern New Mexico. The volcano is Capulin. When we got to the Capulin Volcano National Monument park, we studied the area. Dave wanted to go to the top and walk all the way around the rim. Lita informed us that she was going to stay in the gift shop instead of climbing to the rim. Dave would run ahead and then wait for me to catch up. That was a very unique experience. I suggested that we could also see other sites in the area. We went on to Santa Fe and visited the Loretto Chapel. It has the miraculous stair, which is an unusual helix-shaped spiral staircase. The sisters of Loretto believed that it had been built by Saint Joseph. Later we drove to Albuquerque and rode the Sandia Peak Tramway, the longest aerial tram in America. While riding up to the top of Sandia Mountains, we observed many types of wildlife on the side of the mountain. Our excursion then took us into

Colorado. We toured Denver, Colorado Springs, and the Royal Gorge. Dave and I walked to the center of the Royal Gorge Bridge, which is 955 feet above the river below. We also had the opportunity to ride on the steepest railway in North America.

Kaylie chose Los Angeles as her destination. Our daughter Anjanette accompanied us on this trip. Sites like Disneyland, Universal Studios, and the Chinese Theatre were the order of the days. We also did some window-shopping on Rodeo Drive and took a tour of the movie stars' homes. The Farmers Market provided a change of pace and some good eating. We enjoyed a good meal at Villa Blanca, a restaurant owned by one of the housewives from The Real Housewives of Beverly Hills. We also went to Kyle, a retail store owned by the same housewife. We also went to Santa Monica Pier, where Kaylie and I rode the very tall Ferris wheel. I also accompanied her on her first roller coaster ride; Lita and Anjanette were not up for it. Kaylie also got her picture drawn at the pier. She said it didn't look anything like her. We were also entertained by a skateboarding dog. The dog just kept skateboarding up and down through the crowd.

Our last granddaughter, Meredith, selected New York as her destination. Anjanette also accompanied us on this trip. We went to the Statue of Liberty, Central Park, and the Met. We also ate a hot dog from Gray's Papaya, a place made famous by its mention in the movie Fools Rush In. We laughed at the characters roaming around in Times Square to give you a picture opportunity. The Disney characters posed with Meredith for a picture. Marianela gave one of the characters money for the pose. The others asked for their tip, so Marianela told them that she had given enough for all of them to the first one. By then, the first character was nowhere to be found. A Broadway show was also on our agenda. Once seated, someone from the theater leaned over and told me that I was in an audience-participation seat and asked if I would mind being part of the show. I agreed but didn't tell anyone. They were all surprised when the cast started asking me to sit on stage while they sang to me. Meredith got a big kick out of this.

Life with Marianela was anything but dull. She always managed to provide the energy for any event. But most important of all was that she always dedicated her time to those around her. She fully understood that *time is the only thing you can only spend once.*

# 7

# THE ORDEAL

February 10, 2015, began as any other day for my wife and me. We were going to WinStar Casino to spend the day with some friends as we often did. As usual, we stopped at Cracker Barrel in Denton with three other couples to have breakfast and discuss what we would do with all our winnings.

After we had breakfast, we went on to the casino. Two hours after breakfast, I began to feel uncomfortable. By midafternoon, I felt like I had just finished eating. In fact, I felt like I had overeaten. At about 5:00 p.m., the group wanted to have dinner—that is, everyone except me. I could not even smell food, much less eat it. While the others ate dinner, I had a glass of water with a lime.

Shortly after that, I decided I had to head home to hopefully get some relief. But the more time that passed, the worse I felt. Marianela made the decision to drive me straight to an emergency room. She took me to the Baylor hospital in Frisco because that was the closest to our home.

Doctors performed a scan and determined that I had a blocked intestine. The doctor told me that they would insert a tube into my throat and suction out the contents of my stomach. They tried that but to no avail. We were then told that I would need surgery. My discomfort just kept getting worse.

The next morning, the surgeon informed us that the operating room was being prepared. Marianela asked the surgeon, "How long will the surgery take?"

He replied, "I don't know because I don't know what I'm going to find."

I recall hearing the doctor's comment and not caring how long it took. I just wanted to feel better.

After I was taken to the operating room, I remember the anesthesiologist introducing herself. Shortly after, I entered a state of total relaxation. The surgeon began the operation, and I felt nothing. I was completely out—or so they thought. I felt nothing but heard everything. At one point during the procedure, I heard the anesthesiologist express concern to the surgeon that my blood pressure was extremely low, and she could not control it.

Marianela informed me that the surgery lasted three and a half hours. During the procedure, they removed the part of my small intestine that had the blockage. The doctor told my wife that I would come out of the anesthesia soon and be taken to the ICU. Nelly and our daughters were by my bedside, anxiously waiting for me to wake up. Suddenly the monitors began beeping. The doctors and nurses ran into the room, which was transformed into a scene from *Grey's Anatomy*. Marianela and our daughters, concerned about what they were witnessing, moved out of the way and immediately began praying.

One of the doctors told my family that I was very, very sick, and he did not know if I was going to pull through. He suggested that I be transferred to Baylor in Plano because they had a trauma center and were more prepared to deal with my situation. It seems that about two hours after the end of the surgery, I went into septic shock.

Later, while I was in an unconscious state, I heard the hospital staff talk about my condition. I heard them say that my blood pressure was extremely elevated. They also mentioned that my kidneys were not functioning; they would have to put me on dialysis. My heart was also going into arrhythmia, so they would have to shock it back into rhythm with a defibrillator. My liver was also not working. I was having trouble breathing, so they would have to perform a tracheotomy. My lungs were filling up with fluid, so they were going to have to drain them. It also seemed that I had gallstones; they would have to do a scan to verify that. Hearing all of this stressed me out since I could not utter a single word or even move a finger. All I knew was that things weren't looking good for me.

At that moment, I looked up to a corner of the room and saw my parents, my brother, and our son, all of whom had passed. My mother died at sixty-four of an aneurysm. My father died when he was seventy-three from diabetes complications. Like my dad, my identical twin brother died from diabetes at age sixty-four. Our son passed after living for only two days. The cause of our son's death was determined to be septic shock that developed while he was still in the hospital. The irony was not lost on me; septic shock was now threatening to take my life too.

My father and brother had been on dialysis for several years prior to their deaths. Both lost their vision as a result of diabetes. My father had his legs amputated. However, when I saw both of them in the corner of the room, I was very pleased to see my father's body completely whole. He did not have any limbs missing.

All four of them were about in their early thirties, and their smiles made me feel more at ease during this rather confusing time. I was so happy to see them. I told them that I did not know why I was there and that I did not know what my next step should be. So I asked them to help me take the step intended for me. Without uttering a word, they reassured me that all would be fine and that I should go back. I have never seen faces with such a loving, serene look.

> Lord, hear my prayer; in your faithfulness listen to my pleading; answer me in your justice.
> —Psalms 143:1 (New American Bible Version)

Heavenly Father, how great you are. I am absolutely amazed that you have allowed me to see my loved ones and to know that they are well in your presence. Thank you for the additional time that you have granted me on this earth. I hope to do your holy will so that I may one day join you as well.

It was then that I became aware of my surroundings in the room. Although I was still in an unconscious state, I heard

Marianela's reassuring words comforting me. She told me that I was a strong man. She told me that the church needed me. The Knights of Columbus needed me. The pro-life movement needed me. And above all, my family needed me. She said I should concentrate on getting well. Hearing the word *concentrate*, I realized that the only thing I could control was my mind. I was totally unable to lift a finger or speak. So I began concentrating on all the failing organs mentioned by the caregivers. I focused on my blood pressure, my breathing, my heartbeat, my kidneys, my liver, my gallbladder, and above all, my God.

A few minutes later, the nurse left my room to prepare for my dialysis. Upon her return, she stopped, looked at my catheter bag, and saw that it was filling up with urine. She ran to the nurses' station and asked the other nurse what she had given me because my kidneys were working. The other nurse said she had given me nothing and that she had not even been in my room. When the first nurse entered the room once again, my daughter said it was God answering our prayers. And so, with this miracle, my recovery began.

> *For the Lord will be your confidence and will keep your foot from the snare.*
>                     —*Proverbs 3:26 (New American Bible Version)*

I kept hearing Marianela tell me that all would be fine. She and our daughters began singing spiritual songs to me. Their reassuring voices were very soothing during this stressful time. Marianela said she would sing to me in Spanish since that was my first language. She thought it would be easier for me to understand in my unconscious state. Some of the songs that she sang were "De Colores," "Marinero," "Las Mañanitas," and "El Pescador." My family remained with me throughout this entire ordeal. Given the limitations of the ICU, they entered the room only for a few minutes. However, they kept vigil in the waiting room every day, morning until night.

My wife and daughters were told to head to Baylor in Plano and wait for me to arrive in an ambulance. After they left, I was taken to get an x-ray before being moved to that hospital. I worried that my delayed arrival would be a huge concern for my family. I recall being moved onto a stretcher and taken to the ambulance. I remember the cold air when I left the building to ride in the ambulance, then again when I moved from the ambulance to the next hospital. I realized the urgency of the situation when I heard the siren being used during my transport.

When I arrived in Plano, I kept listening for my family, but it wasn't until several hours later before they were allowed to visit me in the ICU. It took the staff that long to get me situated, connect me to monitors, and get me hooked up to life support. I would be on life support for the next nine days.

Every day my family would arrive, hoping for the best but prepared for the worst. Never having experienced this, they all hoped each day that I would suddenly be back to my old self. One of the ICU nurses noticed their desire to have me make a quick recovery. She came and spoke with Marianela. She told her she firmly believed I would survive this episode but that it would not occur quickly. The nurse said, in her opinion, this would take about three weeks. I was in the ICU two days short of three weeks.

Anjanette wrote this to her mother.

> Yes, baby steps. We prayed for the infection to clear…
> it did! We prayed for him to get the kidney function
> back…he did! We prayed for his heartbeat to become
> regular again…it did! We prayed for his blood pressure
> to stabilize without medicines…it did! We prayed for
> him to wake up and respond…he did! We prayed for
> him to get off the ventilator…he did! We pray that he
> will breathe completely on his own…he will! We pray
> that he will walk around…he will! We pray that he will
> come home healthy…he will!

I was unconscious for about one week during my time in the
ICU. I lost all track of time. When I first recall waking up, I
was told that I had been in the hospital for more than a week. I
thought I had been there only two days. I kept asking what day
it was. Then I would try to calculate the days I had been there;
I guess I thought they were wrong.

During the days I was unconscious, I had many hallucina-
tions that perhaps can be attributed to the medications. It's just
amazing how real they seemed at the time. First, I was totally
convinced that I had been admitted against my will, so the
hospital could charge my insurance. I believed that there was
nothing wrong with me and that I could have gotten up and
gone home if someone would have just driven me.

During another hallucination, Marianela and I had gone
with other couples to the house of one of the couples for a
few days to celebrate Valentine's Day. Unfortunately, the house

had no functioning plumbing. It was being repaired. When I told them that I had to use the bathroom, they said it was no problem because the house was attached to the hospital, and I could just use its facilities. But when I tried to do this, I found myself totally weak and unable to stand. I looked for Marianela to help me, but she was nowhere to be found.

Another time I was convinced that everyone, even the doctors and nurses, went home every night and left me unattended. I could see out the window of my room, or ICU cubicle, and could also see reflections in that window. I was able to see movement behind me because my ICU cubicle had a glass wall facing the nurses' station. Somehow I interpreted this as monsters that were outside staring at me throughout the night.

In a different hallucination, I became aware of some children around me who had no hearts. They were born with a hole where the heart should be. Adults were prejudice against them because of this defect. I tried to talk to the children and convince them that, even if they had no heart, they were loved. They didn't believe me since they often heard mean remarks from the adults. I also tried to convince the adults that the children should be accepted as they were. Also, since I was in the hospital during Valentine's Day, my wife brought me a stuffed animal and placed it on a shelf toward the foot of my bed. Somehow I believed that it too had no heart. There was only a hole where the heart should be. I believed that the children liked my toy dog. When these children saw my dog, they would be joyous to see something they could identify with.

Later, as I was coming out of my unconscious state, I kept asking my wife to take the stuffed dog home. She said she had gotten it for me for Valentine's Day, and it could just stay there. It wasn't until days later when I told her about my hallucination that she took it away. She said she would take it home, but I asked her to please just get rid of it. Our granddaughter is now the proud owner of this stuffed pet.

Because of my condition, I was not allowed to wear my eyeglasses. During the many hours that I spent in my bed, hooked up to all kinds of monitors, I would often be surprised by the various alarms. Every time one would go off, I looked at the screen to see what the problem was. However, without my glasses, even after squinting, it was impossible for me to see. I began judging how critical my situation was by the nurses' response.

After some days of being hooked up not only to monitors but also breathing tubes, feeding tubes, draining tubes. I became aware of how uncomfortable that was. My solution was to remove them all with one quick pull. Talk about alarms and nurses' quick responses! I'd never seen anything like that before. Needless to say, there was blood all over the room. When the nurses saw what my latest altercation had been, they tied my hands down. I soon realized that I would never repeat that, because they had to reinsert every tube again.

I am blessed not only with a very loving family but also with many caring friends. I had so many visitors during the time I was asleep and the time I was awake. I still have people tell me they visited me when I was unconscious, and they are surprised when I tell them I remember their visit.

A good friend of mine from Cuba used to greet me with the words *te quiero y me quedo corto*. He told me it meant that he loved me but that it wasn't enough. When he visited me in the ICU, he used that greeting again. He told me much later that when he said those words to me in the ICU, I began to squirm. I had heard him and wanted to greet him with that same statement, but I was unable to speak. He was surprised to learn that I was aware of his presence; he thought I was unconscious.

Other friends who visited me were the Knights of Columbus. Lupe and Bill would spend countless hours in the waiting room with my family in prayer. At first, my daughters did not know them, but they later became good friends. Bill, to this day, is known to my girls as Uncle Bill. Uncle Bill often brought cookies that he had baked himself. One time he could not find anything to carry them in—other than a Vanity Fair box. His wife was more embarrassed than he was.

When I regained consciousness, I tried to speak, but it was very difficult. My speech was very slurred. I was aware but unable to fix it. My thoughts were also very unclear. I recall telling my wife that I was loopy.

She said, "Yes, Lupe has been here every day with Bill."

I kept repeating that I was loopy, and she kept insisting that Lupe had been there.

I finally pointed to my temple with my finger and moved it in a circular fashion and said, "I'm loopy!"

She laughed indicating that the message had finally been received.

I was also made aware of a problem that I had inadvertently created for my wife. As most couples do, we had a routine. She did certain chores, such as laundry, cooking, etc. I did minor repairs and paid the bills twice a month. I also did most of the computer-related items. Marianela became stressed when she realized she now had to pay the bills. I used a computer program and paid most of them online. Anjanette told her not to worry; she would help her, even if it meant handwriting every check.

The next thing that came up was my scheduled trip to El Paso for the Knights of Columbus. I was in no condition to travel, so they needed to cancel my airline ticket. However, they couldn't do it because they did not know any of my passwords. One of the first things I remember when I regained consciousness was Anjanette asking me for my passwords. Fortunately, I still knew them off the top of my head and wrote them down as soon as I got home.

One of the most difficult things that I had to endure was not being given any water. I spent many days waking up in the ICU and thinking I'd get some water, then ending the day hoping for water tomorrow. I kept asking the nurses for a drink and was told I wouldn't be able to swallow. They were right. One day they gave me a very small piece of crushed ice. I choked on it when I tried to swallow it. I told them if I couldn't have water, perhaps I could have a Shiner Bock. They laughed, nodded, and let me go thirsty.

I remember asking my niece who was visiting from Laredo if she was staying at my house. She was, so I asked her to go to my garage and get me some bottles of water from the refrigerator. I knew I had plenty.

She laughed and said, "*Ay, tío.*"

A few days after being awake, I got tired of being poked and prodded. I began objecting. I even referred to one of the nurses as Nurse Ratched. My wife tried to figure out who that was and kept telling me that I probably meant Miss Hannigan from *Annie*. I kept trying to explain to her who Nurse Ratched was. But I was having trouble talking, and she hadn't seen *One Flew over the Cuckoo's Nest*.

I gave up and said, "Yes, I meant Miss Hannigan."

I even told my wife the nurses were being a pain in my lower back. The nurse said, "I heard that."

I smiled and was glad that she had heard me. It was around this time that they added a remark on my file: *Patient is feisty*.

I was eventually transferred to the Baylor rehabilitation institute in Frisco. The man who drove me asked if I wanted to lie down or sit up during transport. I told him that I was tired of lying down, so I would rather sit. As we got closer to the rehab center, I realized there was a McDonald's one block away. I asked him to go through the drive-through window, and I would pay for both of us. He laughed and turned into the rehab parking lot. I don't know how I would have paid for it since I didn't have my wallet.

I was in rehab for ten days. I was taught to stand, walk, and become fairly independent. The process began when my rehab nurse came in and informed me that I was going for a walk.

I said, "If you say so."

She smiled, helped me to sit up, strapped some sort of belt around my chest, and grabbed it around my back. "OK, on the count of three, you are going to stand up."

I thought she was delusional but figured she knew what she was doing. I heard the count and felt her completely lift me up to a standing position by three. We both waited a few seconds as I regained my balance.

She said, "Let's walk."

I moved one foot forward a few inches, then moved the other one to meet it. I was completely out of breath. I told her that my walk had just come to an end. As she placed me back on the bed, she said it was a good start. I had not realized how much my muscles atrophied after not being used for three weeks.

I will never forget the miracle that our Lord performed. The doctor said I was not going to survive. All my organs were failing. Many patients die of sepsis. Despite all of this, God had other plans. My family and friends stormed the heavens with unceasing prayers. They offered masses and prayed rosaries, the "Chaplet of Divine Mercy," novenas, etc. Their faith did not let them accept the prognostication of the doctors.

We are all aware of the many miracles that God performed years ago. The parting of the Red Sea, the curing of the lepers, and even the raising of Lazarus. If God did those things, then why do we think he stopped performing miracles now? Has he lost his powers? Does he love us less? Of course not. The problem is not that God stopped performing miracles. The problem is that we have become too busy to see and acknowledge them for what they are.

Dear God, never permit me to become blind to your love. May I always be a witness to your glory, Almighty Father, may I always see you in those around me, and may they always see you in me, your servant.

# 8

# THE FAMILY'S REFLECTIONS

Family members wrote their thoughts about this ordeal. This is what they went through during this period.

■ ■ ■

## MARIANELA

How do I start this? What do I say? It is hard even recalling it all.

For a while, Mari, Raul, Anjanette, and I sat quietly, watching the doctors and nurses all work around David. One shot, and another, and another, even to his stomach. My heart was aching, not knowing what was going on but realizing that it was serious. They weren't saying anything, but I could see the worried look in their eyes. I saw the evening nurse, who had taken care of David the previous night, peek his head in the room and just shake his head. Nothing was said; the four of us just remained in the corner, watching everything, not saying anything at all, just praying.

Finally, Dr. Fitzgerald, the head doctor of the ICU at Baylor Frisco, approached us and, with his head down, told us that it didn't look good.

"David has gone into septic shock, and his body is not responding at all," he said.

Although they were doing everything they could, it didn't look good because David was a very sick man. The doctor added that David might not make it through the night. They had done all they could at that location. Because he needed more specialized care, David was getting transferred to the ICU at Baylor's critical trauma center in Plano. The doctor wasn't even sure that David would be able to make it there. He said that he was very sorry! Dr. Fitzgerald was very kind to us. I could see his concern.

Immediately, we hugged each other and started crying. How could this be! It isn't possible! He was fine the day before. I felt so alone. I felt like I was dying with him. I wanted to go with him. I have known him for fifty-three years, and it wasn't enough! We still had so many dreams and plans. We have our beautiful family! So many thoughts went through my head. I felt a sword pierce my heart, just like Our Mother Mary. I could not pray at that moment. All I could say was, "Jesus, help us! Mary, help us!"

All of a sudden, I felt lifted, peaceful, strong—just like in "Footprints"! I told the girls and Raul, "Let's pray." I approached David's bed where he lay so still, almost lifeless. He had a grayish color on his face. When I touched his arm to start praying, I sensed that he was cold and stiff. Yes, it didn't look good at all. But God gave me such strength that I knew could only have come from Him. We prayed. I talked to David. I told him that he was such a strong man and a very positive person. I told him that he could tell his body to start working again. "Tell your kidneys to start working again. Tell your lungs to start working again. Tell your heart to beat in rhythm. Tell your blood pressure to stabilize. Tell your sugar to stabilize." Over and over, I repeated this, praying and singing in between. I sang to him in English; then, thinking that Spanish was our first language, I sang to him in Spanish. I sang "De Colores," "Marinero," "Las Mañanitas." I kept telling him how much I loved him and needed him. I told him how much his daughters, sons-in-law, and grand-children loved him and needed him. I told him he had so much work to do with the Knights of Columbus and the pro-life movement, and they needed him too. I told him that his work on earth was not completed yet. He had so many projects on hand. I reminded him of Meredith's First Holy Communion coming up. I told him he still had to walk Anjanette down the aisle. I told him about the girls' graduation from college com-ing up. I told him that he needed to see Dave become a Knight and knight him personally. So many things came to my mind.

I don't know how I could have done this in such a calm and loving manner. It was all God and Mary by my side. I saw David open his eyes and look around the room, looking up and searching. I knew what that meant. I knew he was seeing his loved ones who had passed! Then he closed his eyes again. And then, so gently, I started to feel some warmth from his arm. His color returned to his face.

A nurse walked into the room and said, "Wow, his kidneys are now working." She ran outside to the nurses' station and brought in the other nurse, asking her, "What did you give him?"

The second nurse responded, "Nothing!"

Anjanette responded, "It's God. We've been praying!"

Oblivious of the time that had transpired, I suddenly realized that I needed to go to the bathroom so badly. I asked Mari to please continue to sing to her dad while I went to the bathroom. I found out that forty-five minutes had passed since I had started talking to him. When I came back, we were asked to go to Baylor in Plano and wait for David to arrive in the ambulance. I asked if I could ride with him, and they said no. They reassured me that there would be two special nurses riding with him, plus all the equipment. By then, David was on life support.

With our hearts broken, we left him behind and headed for Plano. Waiting there for us was Father

Dom, Roger Scott, Karen Garnett, Chacha and Carlos, and Elida and Keco—all very close friends. The ordeal continued. Our faith continued to be tested. David spent nine days on life support, three weeks in ICU, ten days at the Baylor rehabilitation hospital, and two weeks with home health therapists, both physical and occupational. Throughout all this time, we felt loved, cared for, and supported by family, friends, our parish community, the priests, and all the hospital staff. It was indeed quite a journey of love and faith. But most of all, it was a true miracle! God gave him back his life and health! Thank you, God the Father, Jesus, Holy Spirit, Mary, and the numerous saints in heaven.

■ ■ ■

## MARI

One of the most valuable lessons we have received from our parents was watching how they reacted with the loss of Little David. We witnessed the tragedy, shock, pain, anger, love, and healing. Seeing how our parents sought God and his healing hand during life's challenges was the best lesson we could have learned. No matter what life brings, when the storm comes, seek him first, and all else will fall into place.

On February 11, 2015, our family was faced with the possibility of losing Dad. Praying was high on our priority list this time. We all know that one day we will be faced with having to say goodbye to our loved ones, as we all will enter into the other world. When faced with seeing Dad so sick, thoughts vividly raced through our heads. Does he know we love him? Does he know how much he truly means to each of us? Did we say thank you enough times? It is hard to think and question if this is the end of our life with Dad. Dad, if you never knew this before, you are a wonderful father. You did so much for Mom, my sisters, and me, both when we were young and today. We all love you so very much and cannot think of life without you. We do not want to ever take our time with each other for granted. We cherish each and every moment we have together.

This journal is to try to document the days of this storm and how we felt God's glory saw us through it.

May God bless the family and friends who took time to visit and bring us food.

May God bless all the prayer warriors who never ceased to ask and pray for Dad.

May God bless all the families we met in the waiting room, who were also riding their storm with their loved ones.

May God bless the medical team for their true ministry.

Dad, this is what happened while you were sleeping.

I remember coming into the hospital and seeing you in the room on a respirator. A nurse was closely monitoring. Roxanne had just left to pick up the kids, and Mom greeted us and brought us to you.

She said, "Dad, Mari and Raul are here."

It was difficult seeing you down, but we were happy that the surgery was over and you were recovering. Mom and I went to walk around the hospital while Raul stayed with Anjanette in your room. Mom and I walked around for perhaps about fifteen or twenty minutes. When we returned, Raul came to me.

He said, "I think there is something happening. I hear a lot of conversation, and there seems to be more attention placed on your dad."

I sat next to Mom to keep her company. The doctor was in the room and walked to Mom. His face was so grim as he said, "David is very sick. We are doing everything we can do to help, but I recommend that we transfer him to Baylor Plano where the ICU unit can monitor him."

Raul asked him, "Doctor, what does 'very sick' mean?"

The doctor responded, "He has gone into septic shock. It has attacked his kidneys, and they have shut down. This could continue to shut down other organs. We need to move him to the ICU, as this is life-threatening."

Mom was in shock and upset. She cried, saying in Spanish, "Oh my God, if he leaves, I have to leave with him."

I moved the items on the end of the table right next to Mom so I could get as close to her as possible. I put my arms around her and told her, "Mom, we need to pray right now." She seemed to be in a million pieces. She was sobbing in disbelief.

Raul and Anjanette stayed in the room with you, while Mom left the room crying. I followed her out and held her. I remember telling Mom that Jesus was with us this very moment. "His presence is with us now as we all are going through this." We prayed and asked him to cover us with the blood of the lamb and give us the strength to endure the moment. I called Roxanne to let her know what happened and asked her to come back to the hospital.

My next memory was that Mom stormed back into the room with such enormous strength. She appeared so fearful and weak when she left your room but returned so strong. She placed her hands on you and told us all to join her. She began to pray for you, your healing, and your strength. Her prayer was so beautiful. She was filled with his grace.

After she prayed, she began to speak to you. "David, you are not done here. Meredith's First Holy Communion is coming up in May. You are going. Analiese and Roxanne are graduating, and we are going. We are still going to Ireland." She told you, "David, you still have to walk Anjanette down the aisle."

Anjanette quickly interrupted by saying, "Mom, one miracle at a time, please." Would you be surprised that, in the midst of tears and fear, we still had a moment of laughter? Yet another gift you have given to us all.

Mom continued to claim all the future she had planned with you. She then began to sing to you. She always said that she didn't have much of a voice, but she had the most beautiful voice I had ever heard. She sang songs in English and Spanish. I think we had our hands on you for about twenty minutes. It was such a beautiful moment to witness.

After a while, Mom turned to me and told me, "Mari, I have to go to the bathroom. Please continue to sing to your father." So I took over and sang to you. During the whole time that we surrounded you in prayer and song, the medical staff continued working on you.

Shortly after Mom returned, we noticed a commotion again with the medical staff. They began asking each other about medication that had been given to you. They mentioned that your kidneys began working; we all noticed the bag filling up again. Their faces were surprised with wonder about what was given to get the kidneys to function. However, they confirmed nothing had been administered.

Anjanette said, "God did this." Your nurses nodded. What a scary and yet beautiful moment we got to witness. God gave us this miracle. We placed it all in his hands, and we were blessed with the miracle.

Another doctor told us that it was still very serious, and the recovery would be long. The physicians would know more during the next twenty-four hours. Mom asked the doctor if he thought you could survive it. He answered yes, due to your strength and health. He had seen others survive it.

The following days were a series of ups and downs. We were all still in the storm. I remember telling Mom that we did not have the choice about waiting. We had to just wait and see how you were and when you would wake up. We, however, had a choice on how we were going to wait. We could choose to wait in fear or wait in faith.

We chose *faith*.

■ ■ ■

## ANJANETTE

You had just spent your first night at Baylor Frisco. The previous night's decision to drain your stomach was not as successful as the doctor had hoped. Mom stayed overnight at the hospital with you and wouldn't leave your side. You were still in a lot of pain and didn't sleep well. As I was getting dressed for school, I realized that school was not where I needed to be that day. I needed to be at the hospital with you. Roxanne and I headed back to the hospital, only to see you in so much pain. You couldn't sit still and were put on oxygen to help your breathing. The doctors came to let us know that surgery was necessary and was going to be immediate. The intestinal obstruction had to be cleared. Although we were taken by surprise with the quick decision making, we were optimistic that your pain would soon be over. We called Mari to bring her up to date.

We waited patiently while you were in surgery. The doctors later let us know that the surgery went as planned and that the obstruction had been cleared. When it was time for you to leave the recovery room and go back to the room, they asked us to wait in the room right next door. They had already told us that you would be hooked up to many machines, and it would take some time to situate you and the equipment. By that time, Lupe, from Prince of Peace Church, and a man named Bill Webber were also in the room, waiting patiently with us, while you and the hospital team were in the room next door. I don't remember how long it took, but it seemed like a lifetime for us to wait to be able to see you again. I found it interesting that these two men would just sit in silence. None of us had much to say. We just waited and prayed.

By this time, Mari and Raul had decided to head to Dallas to be with all of us.

We were told that we could finally enter the room with you. It was a relief that you were not in pain anymore, but the alternate view was unsettling. You were asleep but surrounded by machines, tubes, screens, IVs, and all the sounds that unnervingly accompany the equipment. It was shocking to take in, but the news was that you were on the mend. We were so grateful, but I remember feeling the need to prepare Mari for what she was going to see when she arrived. I assured her that we were told this was to be expected and that we shouldn't be alarmed.

Later in the day, Mari and Raul arrived. I headed home to let Sprockett out, and Roxanne went to pick up the kids from school and prepare their dinner. It was such a relief that we were all in town now for each other. And it was also as if we had an unspoken pact that Mom would never be left alone.

When I returned to the hospital, the atmosphere was still calm. Mom, Mari, Raul, and I were the only ones at the hospital. I'm not sure of the time frame, but shortly after I arrived, things began to change.

The equipment in the room began to make different sounds. More and more doctors and nurses were entering the room. They had a sense of urgency with their actions and facial expressions. The room was big enough where we could intensely observe without interfering or interrupting. None of us said a word to each other or the medical team. We couldn't take our eyes off the situation. Even without having any medical background or experience, we could still understand enough to know that your health was taking a quick turn for the worse.

Machines were beeping, monitors were showing irregularities, and the medical team was working feverishly to stabilize you. I remember the doctor calling out to the team, "Raise this medicine. Back up on this one. Let's try this…"

Dr. Fitzgerald finally turned to face us, left your bedside, and slowly approached us for the talk. "His system is not reacting as well as we'd hoped. His body has been through a lot. He is a sick man. He is *very* sick, *very, very* sick. We're doing everything we can do right now." The phrase "He is very sick" seemed to replay over and over out of the doctor's mouth.

Raul finally stopped him and said, "You keep saying that he is very sick. What exactly does that mean?"

Dr. Fitzgerald took a pause and said, "I'm sorry. This is life-threatening." There they were—the words we knew had to be delivered.

Mom sat down and immediately began to sob into her own hands. *"No puede ser! No puede ser!"* Mari sat beside her and was holding her as she cried too. The four of us were trying to take in the information and be there for each other as well. As Mom was crying, I heard her say that she wanted to go with you. Mari and I jumped in to stop her from having that thought.

"No, Mom, don't say that!"

I found myself immediately frustrated with the desperation in all of our thoughts. Through clinched teeth, "No! We're not giving up! Dad is still alive and breathing on that bed! It's not over!"

Mom took a second, wiped her tears, and stood up to approach your bedside. She touched your arm and looked at me. Through her tears, "Touch him. He's turning stiff and very cold." I reached out to you and realized she was right.

But…God gave Mom all the strength she needed to help *him* change the situation around. Mom took your hand and began to sing to you. As she was singing, Mari and I stood directly behind her and let our tears fall. She sang and sang. Every now and then, she would stop only to remind you that you still had some things you needed to take care of here on earth.

"David, you said you were going to take me to Ireland!"

Mom then realized that nature was calling, and she needed to go to the bathroom. "Mari, come sing to your father while I go to the bathroom!" When I realized Mom expected us to sing in shifts, I quickly found my seat in the corner by Raul. I figured if anyone would appreciate the spotlight, it would be Mari!

I was amazed that no one in the hospital ever asked us to leave or step out of the room. I now realize that they thought you might have been living your last moments on earth and wanted us to be with you until the very end. But God kept us there for a totally different reason. We were asked to stay so that we could witness and help *him* turn it around. We all continued believing and praying.

One by one, members of the medical team started asking each other, "What did you give him? He's beginning to respond." Nothing had changed in his treatment since Dr. Fitzgerald spoke to us to explain the severity of the situation.

I called out from the corner, "It's because we've been praying."

And so...the miracles began.

■ ■ ■

# ROXANNE

Dad,

Ugh! I have put off writing this letter because I have not wanted to recall the events and memories of that day. It's so hard to do.

I remember asking Mom in the morning how you had slept that night. I was hoping to hear that the nasogastric tube had worked, that you had had relief, that you were on your way to getting better, and that we would be able to get you home in a day or two. Boy, was I wrong! Instead, I heard that you had a horrible night and were possibly going to have surgery. Not what I wanted to hear!

I dropped off the kids at school and headed over to the hospital. When I got there, it was crazy to see a revolving door of nurses coming in and out nonstop and making adjustments to meds, checking your vitals, etc. You were so uncomfortable, and I felt so bad for you. It was hard to see you like that. That was not my strong dad who I know. Mom, Anjanette, and I were just sitting back silently and watching, praying, and not knowing what to think. I just felt helpless.

When talking to one of the nurses, he mentioned that you were going to have surgery. We were surprised. We knew it was a possibility, but we hadn't been told that it was a sure thing. We asked him when, and he said, "Now! The operating room is being prepped."

He said the doctor was going to be in to talk to us, and it felt like forever before that happened. Dr. Cribbens came in and let us know what he was going to do. Mom mentioned to him several times about how much you like hot sauce and that she wanted you to stop eating it. He just kept laughing and asked, "She just will not let that go, will she?"

We laughed and said, "No, she won't."

Right before they wheeled you back, the chaplain, Christine, came by. She talked to us and prayed with us. She was so sweet and kept checking in with us the entire time we were there.

Mom, Anjanette, and I just sat and waited while you were in surgery. Chacha, Carlos, Elida, and Keco came to visit, as well as Bill and Lupe. Shortly after they all arrived, we were told you were out of surgery and that everything had gone well. They said you would be sedated and on the ventilator for at least twenty-four hours. They also said that you were very sick and that you would need your rest.

Everyone left but Bill and Lupe. This was the first time I had met either of them. They sat quietly talking to each other. Lupe left the room to call Prince of Peace and see if Father Dom could come to visit. He

came back in and said he would be visiting later, and
he left. Bill just sat in the chair at the foot of your bed,
silently. He didn't say anything. I just kept watching
him, wondering how he knew you, how close you two
were, etc. He just seemed content to be sitting there in
silence.

I had to leave to pick up the kids from school. I
kept waiting because I was hoping to catch Mari and
Raul before I left, but I didn't get to. They were pulling in as I was leaving, so I just missed them, but I
was glad that they were there with Mom and Anjanette
while I was gone. My plan was to pick up the kids, get
them home for a snack and homework, and then head
back to see you. However, when I called to check up
on you and let them know I was headed back, Mari
said to wait because you were going to be transferred
to Baylor Plano. I asked why, and she said that you had
had some complications earlier and that Baylor Plano
was a trauma hospital that would be better for you.

I really didn't understand what had happened,
but she sounded preoccupied, so I just let her go and
waited. About an hour or so later, it was about 7:30
p.m., and I hadn't heard anything. Nathan had gone to
New York that day, so the kids were going to be left
home alone. I didn't know how late I could stay, so I
just headed to Baylor Frisco.

When I got there, everyone looked exhausted and
worried. Mari and Anjanette updated me on what had
happened earlier that day, and I was so shocked. I

didn't know what to think. I just tried to comprehend it all and prayed as we waited to find out when you would be transferred. I just wondered about the events. *Why is this happening? What did you see? What did you hear? Did you see Uncle Dan? He had to be with you!* I just kept praying to him and to God.

Shortly thereafter, they said they were ready to transfer you, and we left for Plano. I called Nathan on my way. He was with his coworker in the car. He asked me how you were, and I just started bawling, saying, "I don't know how he is!" I just lost it. I told him what had happened and that we almost lost you.

We got to the ICU waiting room. It was full of people, a family for one of the other patients. We made our way to a little corner of the room. Who knew that would be our spot for the next month? Chacha and Carlos brought us sandwiches and cookies, since none of us had eaten dinner. Keco and Elida showed up too, and so did Karen, a Catholic pro-life community lady, as well as Father Dom. We just sat there waiting for you to get there, and Father Dom led us in the rosary. It was getting late, and people started leaving. Karen stayed with us, and we finally got to see you around 11:00 p.m. Karen, Mom, Mari, Anjanette, and I all went in. Karen led us in a prayer, and we sang the "Divine Mercy Chaplet." It was so peaceful and a nice way to end the day, under the circumstances.

We left the hospital with relief that the day was over, with worry of what the coming days would bring, and with the faith that God could bring us through it. I realize that, as challenging and sad as that day was, it was not the day we almost lost you. It was the day God gave you back to us, and I will be forever grateful!

Love you,
Roxanne

■ ■ ■

# ANALIESE

On February 11, 2015, I woke up to a text message from my mom saying that you were not feeling well and having exploratory surgery. I just laid there in confusion. I started to pray, asking him to heal you and to be with the medical staff that was performing the surgery. Knowing that my parents were going to leave during lunchtime, I was becoming fearful but continued to pray. I went to school and ran straight to my mom's office. She had already left. I immediately started crying and wondering what was going on. *Why was this happening? Is it fixable?* I went back to my apartment and lay in bed, thinking of every single memory I had of you—all of the wonderful, great, and funny memories. I went to work, and that is when I received the text message about the infection. I left work and just sat in my car. Every message was very vague because no one was really sure what was going on or how to break the news to us, especially knowing that we were all in school and in San Antonio.

My dad later texted Mamu and Papu (the other grandparents) to communicate your health updates. Mamu called me shortly after. I cried and cried to her on the phone. She told me that you knew how much I loved you and that you would not want me to miss school or work. She prayed with me on the phone. After our conversation, I went back to my apartment. I was alone because it was Roxanne's busy Valentine's weekend at Edible Arrangements, and Lauren was at the dorm. Everyone in San Antonio kept calling me to see if we were OK and ask for updates. I asked every ministry that I was involved in to pray for you. There are never enough prayers. In return, I told all the people that I would pray for their intentions. I know that my mom and aunts were taking care of Lita, and I knew I had to be there for Roxanne, Lauren, Dave, Kaylie, and Meredith. I texted them to make sure they were OK, to make sure they knew that *you* were going to be OK, but all we could do was pray.

We were able to travel to Dallas the next weekend. I was preparing myself to see you. I was not excited to be there only to make sure that I was able to tell you that I loved you. I was not sure if I was going to get another opportunity to do so. My dad prepared Sanny and me as we were walking into the room. You were lying there, but as soon as we told you it was us, you immediately started moving your arms and tried so hard to open your eyes. I started crying because I knew you understood. In my psychology classes, I had learned about how amazing the brain is and how sometimes people can recall what happens. When I finally saw my mom, I told her, "Papa David has an exceptional, brilliant brain. I have read about this. He is going to be able to recall everything. I know it!" If she believed me or not, I don't know, but I had faith that you could do it.

The progress you made was beyond amazing. Every step was a success. All of us came together as a team and decided that *you* were going to be OK. Why God had this in our plan, we do not know, and maybe we will never understand. But it has taught me to never take life for granted because things can change so quickly.

I love you, and I will always cherish every memory with you. You have been the most amazing grandfather. I thank God for you every single day.

I am ready to be a part of a not just good but great, outstanding year with you.

Analiese

■ ■ ■

## SANNY

I remember that like it was yesterday, being at work and getting a text from Mom saying they were leaving to Dallas because you had gotten sick. At the time, I was working at Edible Arrangements, and it was our biggest holiday of the year. I had gotten the text late, and I did not know what was going on. Trying to keep up with everyone's texts while being stuck at work was one of the hardest things. As the texts kept coming in, I did not really understand what was going on. I was scared and clueless. I just went to the restroom and started crying. I was upset because I wasn't able to be there, and I did not know what was going on. My parents did not tell us much detail until they came back to San Antonio.

The following weekend we were all able to go visit. I remember telling my parents that I did not want to go inside your room. I had seen one picture of you, and I knew that there was no way I wanted to see you in person. I did not want to see you until I saw my Papa David again—the Papa David who made us laugh at any moment, the Papa David who would sit on the couch and use his phone, the Papa David who would tell us interesting stories about new inventions, the Papa David who did everything and anything just to see his grandchildren smile. Seeing the picture of you was one of the hardest things I had to look at. I was not strong enough to walk in that room and keep myself together. I did not want you to see me breakdown. I knew all you needed was happy smiles.

We soon arrived at the hospital. When we parked in the parking garage, I had gathered all my thoughts and courage and decided that I was going to go in and see you. There was no way that I was not going to go in that room. I needed to keep it together for you. I wanted you to know that I loved you and that I was there just like everyone else. Walking in that room and looking into your eyes, I felt as if you did not even know who I was. I was scared and upset because I did not want you to go. I wasn't prepared to lose you. I prayed, held your hand, and you just stared at me. I could see it in your eyes that you wanted to say something, but you just could not.

The second time I went in there was when I said to myself, "Yep, that's my Papa David!" Mom, Lita, Roger, and I were trying to talk to you, and you kept whispering something. No one could understand what you were saying, and in my head, I remember thinking that you said you wanted a Shiner Bock. But I was like, no, I'm too embarrassed to guess what you were saying because I did not know if I was wrong. You kept repeating it over and over again, and then I whispered to Mom, "I think he is saying he wants a Shiner Bock." Mom immediately blurted it out, and you smiled nodding your head. From that moment, I knew—that's my Papa David making jokes!

Sunday was our last day before we had to head back to San Antonio. Everyone said their goodbyes, coming back and forth from seeing you and sharing your words in the waiting room. Everyone was laughing because you kept asking for all these drinks. Erika and I were the very last people to say goodbye. I was excited because I knew I was going to get to say good-bye to my Papa David. When we walked in, it was like a complete switch. There were no jokes being said. You just kept shaking your head and closed your eyes. Erika was trying to talk to you, and you just kept shaking your head, as if you were saying no to us. We did not know what was going on because everyone had all these funny stories, and within a matter of minutes, you weren't the same. From what I understood, you kept saying that you wanted to give up and that you were tired.

Erika kept saying in Spanish, "No, you are not going anywhere. You need to see Sanny graduate, and you have to be at my wedding."

All you kept doing was shaking your head as if you were saying no. Erika and I were sad and confused. We said our goodbyes, and as we were walking away, Erika and I stopped in the hallway and cried. We didn't want anyone to see us crying, and we did not know what to tell the family. We didn't have a funny story, but I also did not want to scare anyone either and tell the family what you were doing when we were talking to you. Everyone was so happy that you were making jokes with them. I did not want to scare anyone, especially Lita. I cried the whole way on the drive back to San Antonio. I did not know what to think.

A couple of days later, I was happy to hear my mom share about your progress. As the weeks passed, you kept getting better and better. I thank God every day for your life. I love you so much, Papa David.

You later said, "I didn't get off life support for a *good* year. I got off life support for an *outstanding* year!" Cannot wait to make more memories with you, Papa David.

Sanny

# 9

# REHABILITATION AND HOMECOMING

In the rehabilitation center, I was taught everything that used to come naturally to me. I was taught to speak and move my arms and legs. I was confined to a wheelchair for days. At first, I propelled myself by using my arms to move the wheels. Later, in order to strengthen my legs, I was told to propel myself by partially walking while sitting down. As my legs got stronger, I was upgraded to a walker. Several times a day, I took walks with the help of the walker and the rehab technician. First my walks were only in the room. Later I started going up and down the hallways. Eventually I was taken outside and taught how to maneuver the walker on curbs and other uneven surfaces.

One day I recall the rehab technician allowing me to cross the parking lot and go as far as the sidewalk. I asked if I could cross the street, and she said no. I told her that was a good answer; if she had allowed me to cross the street, I would be gone, never to return.

To help me regain my strength, they would have me fold clothes on a tall table. This improved my arm mobility, and, since I was standing up for some time, it also strengthened my legs. We were also asked to play games like Jenga or Scrabble while standing. When the technician told me that she wanted me and another patient to play Jenga, I told her that I refused. I informed her that my hands shake involuntarily, and I would not be able to move the pieces properly. We decided that Scrabble would be a better option. After some time of playing a lady opponent, she informed me that one time when she played Scrabble, she had gotten a real bad case of diarrhea. I quickly finished the game, declaring her the winner, and went back to my room.

Later I was escorted to a set of three wooden steps with handrails. I was assigned the task of climbing them. During my first try, I was only able to go up on the first step, turn around, and come back down one time. My legs were shaking, and I was totally out of breath. Later I was able to go up to the top step and come back down several times.

There were many patients in the rehab center. Some were having a harder time than me. I would try to encourage them by telling them that the pain was only temporary. One of my granddaughters surprised me with a pair of superhero socks. In the area that would cover my shins was the Superman logo. On the back were two long strips that would fly as Superman's red cape. I'm glad that the socks gave everyone laughs and encouraged them to keep going.

Before being sent home, I was asked to walk out of my room, go down the hall all the way to the kitchen, and come back. To prove to the technician that I had accomplished this, I had to tell her what was on the menu that day. When I returned, I told the tech that today they were serving *vichyssoise* and *duck à l'orange*. She looked at me, puzzled, wondering where I had gone! I told her it was the same old boring tacos. She approved my discharge.

On the day of my dismissal, Marianela drove the car to the front door of the rehab center. The staff helped me into the car and waved goodbye. Once home, Marianela helped me out of the car and into the house through the garage since that path had no steps. I was still dependent on a walker.

For a few weeks, two different therapists visited me at home to help me with my various exercises. One of the therapists took me outside my house. The first time, I was only able to walk the distance of one house and back. Gradually, with her help, I was able to increase the distance until I could walk across the front of ten houses and back. Every day I felt stronger and more convinced that soon I would be back to normal.

Some days later Marianela took me to the mall so I could take a walk while having a different view. I was only able to walk from the center to one end and back, and that's after having to sit down to catch my breath.

I must add that I was able to attend my granddaughter's First Holy Communion, as my wife had told me that I had to get well for. I also was able to be present at my other granddaughter's college graduation. God is good.

I am forever grateful to God, to my family and friends, and to Marianela who has always been my rock. She has always manifested a true faith in our Lord, to our family and those around us.

Thank you, God, for allowing me more time so that I can continue to support my family and be there for them. May your will be done. Amen.

# 10

# THANKSGIVING

Some months later a friend of ours was admitted to Baylor Scott & White in Frisco for back surgery. Marianela and I went to visit him and his wife after the surgery. This was the same hospital where I had my intestinal surgery. The next day our patient friend called and told me there was a doctor who asked about me. He wanted to know if I would be back to visit my friend and, if so, if it would be possible for me to see him. My wife and I were totally confused but told him that we would be there that afternoon. When Marianela and I walked on the floor, we saw Dr. Fitzgerald. He came to me and hugged me.

He said, "You are a true blessing."

This was the doctor who had told Marianela and my daughters that I was very sick and would not make it. I guess God had other plans.

One day during my recovery at home, Marianela asked if I could help with her homework. She had been taking a Bible study class on our Blessed Mother. I agreed to help her. As she mentioned various Bible verses, I read them and reflected on them as they related to her class. She asked me to read Luke 1:46–47. This is known as the Canticle of Mary.

*Visiting Elizabeth shortly after the Annunciation, Mary said, "My soul proclaims the greatness of the Lord; my spirit rejoices in God my Savior."*

Having read these words, I remained silent. Marianela asked me, "What's wrong?"

I said nothing was wrong. I had just been amazed at these words. They reflected exactly what was going on in my life. My soul—my very being—proclaims the greatness of the Lord. It is due to God that I am here this very minute. Thank you, God.

When the angel Gabriel came to Mary in Luke 1:28, he greeted her, "Hail, favored one. The Lord is with thee." Mary must have been confused.

Yet in Luke 1:38, she pondered the greeting and said, "Behold, I am the handmaid of the Lord. May it be done to me according to your word." What an impact those words had on humanity. Similarly, we too have choices in our daily lives. We don't know what the impact of our choices are, but we should always say yes to God. I must admit that most of the time, my prayers comprise requests of God. It seems that I am always asking for something. Sometimes I get what I want; sometimes I don't. But the only time that I get what I ask for is when I ask for God's will to be done. Mary's answer to Gabriel should be ours as well.

Marianela and I have accepted God's will throughout our lives. Sometimes his will for us gives us happiness—sometimes sorrow. But in all cases, we have seen his glory and felt his love.

One of my favorite sayings is *God leads by closing doors*. When we lose a job, an opportunity, or a thing, I always look for what God is giving us to take its place. And without fail, the replacement is better. I believe this is God's way of nudging us when we become complacent. He wants us to move on to a better place.

Several times in my career, I have applied for a job or a promotion, only to find out that either the job was eliminated, or the company was dissolved. God had closed that door.

None of us know why we are anywhere at any time, but I have to believe that God has us here for a reason. Years later I understood why I was still on this earth.

# 11

# ANNIVERSARY CRUISE

In spring 2017, our daughters began asking us how we wanted to celebrate our fiftieth wedding anniversary. Marianela immediately said that instead of a party, she would rather have all of us go on a cruise. The planning started right away. We searched online to determine the destination, dates, pricing, etc. Once the dates were set, everyone put in for vacation time.

The ladies began shopping for dresses and bathing suits. The men purchased suntan lotion and other items. We had a countless number of conversations leading up to this event. If someone became aware of an upcoming special sale, we all knew about it. The closer the trip got, the more excited we all became. My daughter Roxanne got us all T-shirts and stenciled *Papa David and Lita's 50th Wedding Anniversary, 06.10.17* on the front. The back of Marianela's shirt read *Lita,* and the back of mine read *Papa David.* We all wore them as we boarded the ship, and everyone kept congratulating us. That was fun!

Our cruise departed from Galveston, Texas, on June 3 and returned on June 10, the actual day of our anniversary. We all met in Galveston on June 2 and spent the night. We were not going to take any chances of missing the boat. The next day we all met for breakfast and headed to the pier.

When we boarded and got to our cabin, we saw that it had been decorated with many items wishing us a happy anniversary. Our family had provided us a cake too. What a thoughtful and pleasant surprise!

Our first stop was Cozumel, Mexico. Of course, shopping was the order of the day. Lita took us away from the pier; she did not want to stay in the tourist area. She told us the farther away that we got from there, the better the bargains. She was truly an amazing shopper; everyone relied on her expertise. After a few hours shopping, we went to an outdoor restaurant to have a late lunch and relax.

Our second stop was beautiful Belize. We had a relaxing day at the beach, enjoying the crystal-clear blue water of the Caribbean. The grandkids went on a banana boat with their father. Lita and I just waved at them, took pictures, and ordered another cold beer. It didn't get any better than that.

Our third stop was Roatán, Honduras. This was an interesting stop. We took a tour of the town, which included a chocolate factory, a metal decorations shop, and an iguana farm. The chocolate factory was interesting but uncomfortably hot since it had no air-conditioning. The metal decorations shop provided us an opportunity to purchase souvenirs. At the farm, we were told about this lady that loved iguanas, so she got two of them. She kept feeding them, and they kept multiplying. At the time of our visit, there were more than a thousand iguanas at that location. I thought Marianela was going to be scared and avoid them. We were all surprised when she carefully stepped over them...just to get to the gift shops. She's a real trooper.

Fifty years earlier, when I had seen Marianela walk up the aisle over the rose petals, I never would have imagined that I would see her walk up the sidewalk, carefully stepping over the iguanas. We never know what life has in store for us.

On our way back to the ship, we encountered two men playing local music on a marimba. The older of the two men reminded us of Marianela's father. Anjanette said hello to him, and before you knew it, she had joined the group. And no, she doesn't know how to play, but that made no difference.

Two nights before the end of our cruise, we had the captain's dinner. This was a formal affair. By now, we had gotten to know our waiters and vice versa. My grandson was always served two desserts, and my youngest granddaughter, Meredith, was always asked to join them in their dance. This time our six grandchildren sang to our waiters. They thoroughly enjoyed it and told us, through all the years they had worked on the ship, this was the first time anyone ever sang to them.

Lita and I are so grateful to all our family for making this possible. We will never forget this anniversary cruise and all the memories we made.

# 12

## DECLINING HEALTH

Three months after our cruise, in September 2017, Marianela began having some health issues. She went to her doctor and was diagnosed with a urinary tract infection. She was prescribed an antibiotic, and the infection disappeared. But once she ended the medication, the infection returned. This happened several times. At this same time, she also complained of joint pain. She was sent to a rehabilitation center with the hope that she would get better. Marianela also got shingles on the inside of her left arm. The doctor informed us that she had developed them even though she got the shingles vaccine.

As a result, the holidays were very difficult. She was the one that always prepared the Thanksgiving feast. And, believe me, it was not just a meal; it truly was a feast. This year it was very different. She only baked a couple of pies. The turkey and the sides were prepared by other family members while she sat on her lounger and observed. Never had I seen her like that.

Our grandson's birthday was on December 15. It was so heart-wrenching to see her celebrate with the family in her weakened state. As much as she tried to cover up what she was going through, it was apparent to all of us that her health was declining.

During the following days, she continued to get worse. Her strength diminished daily, so she returned to the doctor. The blood work results were devastating. On December 19, we were told that they suspected that she had acute myeloid leukemia (AML). A dagger stabbed through my heart would have inflicted less pain than that diagnosis. We were both stunned. All we could do was hold each other and weep. *Now what?*

On the subsequent Sunday, I attended Mass. After Mass, I was greeted by our friends as usual. They asked me about Marianela since her weakened state had prevented her from going to church. I broke down and cried as I told them the news. Our friends who had been by her side while she dealt with my health issues were now with me as I dealt with hers.

December 23 was our daughter's birthday. I tried to persuade Marianela to tell the family about her health issues. She wouldn't hear of it. She wasn't about to spoil these days for the family. She insisted that we would tell them after Christmas. I recall going to our daughter's house for her birthday dinner. My darling wife was lying down on the sofa, completely drained of energy. She was able to get up just long enough to eat. As soon as we ate, she asked me to take her home. We had been invited to a Christmas Eve dinner. We declined to attend and just told everyone else to go on with their plans. Little did we know what lay ahead.

On Christmas morning, I saw Marianela so weak that she was unable to stand. Anjanette came over, with her puppy, to prepare breakfast for us. She was concerned because her dog was jumping all over her mom. Anjanette could only kneel next to her and cry. Over the past few days, Anjanette had gone to various restaurants to get her mother meals to eat. One time she went to get a smoothie for her and asked them to add as many vitamins as they could. Once Anjanette saw her mother's condition, she called her sister to come over—alone. Once she arrived, I informed them that I was taking their mother to the hospital. We practically had to carry her into the car given her weak state.

Marianela suggested that we take her to Baylor Scott & White in Plano. She had grown to like them during the time that I had been there in 2015. The medical staff immediately began running tests. She was extremely anemic. They called for a gastroenterologist, who soon determined that she did not have internal bleeding. All other tests pointed to the AML as the cause of her problem. She was given blood transfusions, which strengthened her a bit.

Anjanette and Roxanne went downstairs to the cafeteria and decided to call their sister, Mari, in San Antonio. They dreaded having to tell Mari that the diagnosis was leukemia. Mari told them that she would be heading to Dallas.

After two days in the hospital, the doctor suggested we go home and pack her a bag so she could stay in the hospital long-term. They also suggested that we go to the Baylor in Dallas since they had a better oncology department. The oncologist made an appointment for her admittance into the downtown hospital.

During the two days, we not only prepared our suitcases, but we also prepared ourselves and our family for what was to come. Mari came up to be with us from San Antonio. Following my GPS, we all headed to downtown Dallas. But once there I realized that I was still lost. The medical complex is so large that we had to stop while Mari went into a gift shop to ask for directions.

We were directed to the T. Boone Pickens Cancer Hospital. I was completely astonished by the fact that an entire hospital was dedicated to serve only cancer patients. After going through the preliminary registration process, we were escorted to Marianela's room on the fifth floor.

The medical staff immediately hooked her up to monitors and equipment that would be used for her treatments. The family was asked to step out for a short time while a specially trained nurse came in to place a PICC line. Later we all learned that this three-tube device, placed on the inside of her upper arm, was to be used to draw blood and infuse whatever things she needed. This would allow everything to be done without having to constantly poke her. The placement of this apparatus required that the arm be penetrated, so we were asked to leave the room to avoid any contamination.

Once we were allowed back into her room, our daughters immediately began transforming that space into Marianela's new home. They hung pictures that were very meaningful to all of us. They placed a calendar on the wall and marked special family events to ensure that we would not miss them. They also wrote down what their mom was going through on any one day.

New Year's Eve was a few days after her hospital admission. In preparation for this, my sons-in-law reserved rooms in a nearby hotel. They requested rooms facing downtown so we could see the fireworks. Early in the evening, we celebrated with Marianela in the hospital. We had bought nonalcoholic champagne for the toast. Marianela fell asleep early, so we went to the hotel and waited for the fireworks to begin at midnight. However, all that was visible of the fireworks were small flashes of light, barely visible between the buildings. We ended up seeing the fireworks on television.

Marianela's sister called to wish us all a happy New Year and informed us that she and her family would be coming up from Laredo. Marianela asked her to bring with her two *roscas de reyes*, which are king cakes. One was for us; the other was for her nurses. The Feast of the Epiphany is celebrated on January 6. This is when the three kings arrived at the manger with their gifts for the Christ child. When Marianela saw the nurses, she gave them the king cake and explained its tradition. There is a tiny plastic baby somewhere inside the cake, and whoever gets the piece of cake with the baby throws the next party. The nurses were very grateful.

We quickly learned the hospital routine. Blood was drawn at 4:00 a.m., and results came at 7:30 a.m. Breakfast was served at 8:00 a.m. Corrective procedures followed. Blood and/or platelet transfusions would be administered depending on her test results from that morning.

We had been told that she would be starting a chemotherapy regimen, but nothing was administered right away. On about the third or fourth day, we learned that the reason nothing had been administered was that they were running a battery of tests to determine the exact type of AML that she had. This would allow them to find the most effective chemotherapy for her.

The doctor had an allergy or a cold; either way, he wore a mask when he entered the room. This was all new to us and made us a bit uncomfortable—but not as uncomfortable as the message he delivered. He walked up to a whiteboard and began writing on it. Nothing made any sense to any of us. He pointed to the name of a medicine and explained that, when administered, it would get rid of her cancer. He then pointed to another medicine and said that one was much milder; it would not cure her cancer, but it would allow her to live two or three years before the cancer would take over. He asked us to decide whether to use the first or the second one.

"I've got to tell you that the first one will cure the cancer, if it doesn't kill you," he said to Marianela.

He informed us that, given Marianela's age, this could be a real problem. By now, we had forgotten the uneasiness we felt about his mask. We all looked at each other and told Marianela it was her decision to make; we would support her either way.

She said a quick prayer, took a deep breath, and replied, "Let's go for the total cure."

And so the next phase began.

*I can do all things through God who strengthens me.*
      *—Philippians 4:13 (New American Bible Version)*

I recalled the look on our daughters' faces when they learned of their brother's passing. It reflected concern and confusion. But their faces also showed love for one another. I now saw that same look and that same love.

Almighty Father, we reach out to you in this time of need, in this time of uncertainty. Please continue to guide us through this with your love. Help us to accept your holy will. Amen.

# 13

## TREATMENT BEGINS

Besides getting rid of her cancer cells, the chemotherapy could produce many side effects for Marianela. We were told she would lose her hair. She would be nauseous. Her red blood cell and platelet levels would decrease. Due to a lower white blood cell (WBC) count, her bodily defenses would become weaker. We were instructed to let the nurses and doctors know if any of these symptoms were present so they could give her medications to reduce discomfort.

Every day they drew blood early in the morning and wrote down the results for us on a whiteboard. They created a handwritten spreadsheet that listed the various results for that particular date. This would allow us to keep track of how things were progressing—or not. Early on, these numbers were nothing but hieroglyphics to us, but we soon began understanding them. The doctors explained them to us when they made their rounds.

Every day we would anxiously await those numbers, anticipating the changes that we had been told would happen. It wasn't until the fourth or fifth day that we began to see the lowering of the blasts (cancer cells). We also began to see lower hemoglobin (HBG), platelet, and WBC numbers. Decreased HBG made Marianela anemic and weaker. A platelet depletion meant her blood would not coagulate, and it also caused bruises all over her body. A lower WBC compromised her defenses, making her neutropenic.

At the same time, Marianela began seeing much of her hair show up on her pillowcase. This reminded me of the many times that I went out with her to parties. Her hair was always impeccable. When our dates were for dances or other special occasions, she would go to a beauty salon. I never saw her with a single hair out of place. Even after we were married with children and grandchildren, she always looked so prim and proper. As soon as she saw the slightest gray hair, she would color it.

Now here it was, her perfect hair falling out on her pillow. It saddened me because I could only imagine how much it meant to her. Some days later she asked the nurse if there was anyone who could come and shave her head. They did not know of anyone but told her not to worry—soon it would all be gone. The next day she asked another nurse to shave her head. She was willing to do it, but she also wanted her to know that she had never done that for any other patient. A few minutes later, the job was done. I looked at her and realized how beautiful she still was. I used to tell her she looked more beautiful every day. That day was no exception.

Sometime later Marianela's cancer cells were at zero. Unfortunately, so were her white blood cells, which meant she had absolutely no immunity. We were extremely careful to ensure that she would not get infected in any way. The nurses would administer anti-nausea medicine, blood transfusions, and platelet transfusions whenever necessary. The blood transfusions would bring her HBG count up for two or three days, then she would need more blood.

When her first round of chemotherapy was completed, we kept looking at those numbers. Her HBG would drop, and she would get another transfusion. The two numbers that kept us spellbound were the blasts and the WBC. Fortunately, the blasts continued at zero...but unfortunately, so did the WBC. Twenty-one days after her chemotherapy ended, we began seeing a slight increase in her WBC. Every day we saw them slowly rise, which meant she was beginning to regain her immunity. Her blasts stayed at zero. Every day we would hold our breath and expect the best. We took a picture of the new numbers on the whiteboard every day and texted them to our family, thanking them for their prayers and support. It seemed that she had survived the chemotherapy that she was told might kill her. *Thank you, God.*

Days later we were told that it was time for a second round of chemotherapy to begin. *Oh, not again...*

The doctors and nurses informed us that this round would be slightly lighter than the first. They were right; the side effects were less intense. Her numbers dropped but recovered much more quickly. She required fewer blood and platelet transfusions, and her WBC did not drop to zero. The other good news was the cancer cells were still gone.

Another doctor began visiting us. She introduced herself as the bone marrow transplant specialist. She informed us that Marianela would need a bone marrow transplant in order to prevent the return of those miserable blasts. Unknown to us, they had already started looking for a bone marrow donor for her. Our three daughters immediately got tested and were only a 50 percent match. This was to be expected since half of their DNA came from Marianela, and the other half came from me. As the hospital searched for a higher match, we were told to go home and recover from her six-week hospital stay.

# 14

# BONE MARROW TRANSPLANT

During her stay at home, Marianela still had to visit the oncologist. At first, it was on a daily basis, then every other day. They would do blood work every time and send us to another area for transfusions when necessary. When she needed two blood transfusions, our visit would exceed six hours. But we were still glad to be going home each time.

In addition to her daily doctors' visits, we had to attend a seminar with our family members. This seminar was to teach us about the life ahead for Marianela and for us. Early on, the doctor informed us that this was not a sprint; it would be a marathon. Therefore, we were prepared for recovery to take a long time. I asked her bone marrow transplant doctor what we could expect at the end of this marathon. Would it be life as usual? She said that, although we would get back to normal, it would be a new normal. We should expect Marianela to feel tired more often and to probably need daily naps. The finish line would mean that she would have lived her next five years cancer free. All of us were ready to see her get across the finish line.

The search for a matching donor, led by Be The Match, was a complicated process. One day we were informed that they had found a 100 percent match. A 100 percent match? Who was this donor? It turned out that Be The Match searched their international file of volunteer donors and found a young man in Brazil that was a perfect match. Thank you, God.

*With God, all things are possible.*
          —*Matthew 19:26 (New American Bible Version)*

Now that they found a donor, the doctors told us that Marianela would have to undergo testing to verify that she was strong enough for the next phase of chemotherapy. This next phase would be the strongest yet. We drove to the hospital daily to undergo different tests. Her lungs were tested. Her heart was tested. Her blood was tested. This last test showed that the blasts were still at zero—no cancer cells. They could not proceed with the transplant if the cancer had returned. Since she passed all the tests, we were asked to admit her to the hospital again.

When we were in the admissions office, we ran into a young lady who had attended the seminar with us earlier. We asked if she was being admitted for her bone marrow transplant, and she said her cancer had returned, so she was not able to proceed to the transplant yet. She was being admitted to undergo another round of chemotherapy.

This time Marianela was admitted to a different floor—the bone marrow transplant floor. This space was exceptionally clean. When we got off the elevator, we noticed that there was a process before entering the patient area. Everyone had to place their face on a monitor to ensure that you did not have a fever. Then we had to pass through two sets of doors. Each room had a separate air-conditioning system to avoid cross contamination. Other than that, everything else seemed the same as the rooms during her previous stays.

By then, her hair had started growing back. It was gray with some areas of black. But this time, it was curly. She was so happy to have it come back; however, for special occasions she wore a wig that resembled her previous look. The last time she wore it was when she took pictures with our grandson in his cap and gown to commemorate his high school graduation. We went to the front of the school and took pictures with him. She dressed up with pearl earrings and a pearl necklace. She was so proud of our grandson, and we were all so proud of her.

When she was admitted in April, Marianela was given a full-body radiation treatment to ensure that there were absolutely no cancer cells left. Then came the chemotherapy. The administration of that next chemo treatment caused her beautiful hair to fall out again. Since she didn't complain, it didn't seem to bother her, but I'm sure it secretly did. How could it not?

This round of chemotherapy was devastating. She was given medicine to help with her nausea. Blood transfusions would build her up slightly, but the loss of platelets caused her to have bruises all over her body again. At one time, she even got a nosebleed that took hours to get under control. And again my beautiful girl never complained. We were all amazed at her strength and faith that she exhibited daily.

Blood analysis and a bone marrow biopsy confirmed that she was still cancer free. *Thank you, God.* The bone marrow donor was contacted, and May 9, 2018, was the date set for the donation. A few days before, the donor was given some injections that would stimulate his body to produce more bone marrow than usual. On May 9, the donor gave his bone marrow in a hospital in Brazil, and it was immediately packaged in a special container and flown to Dallas. I understand that the container with the bone marrow flies in the cockpit with the pilot.

The precious cargo was tested as soon as it arrived at the Dallas hospital. On May 10, a nurse brought in the much-awaited donation. Along with the chaplain, all of us prayed over the bag prior to Marianela receiving it. She was then administered the bone marrow. It looked like a blood transfusion, with one exception. The bone marrow cells are actually large enough that they are visible to the human eye. They looked like minuscule grains of sand suspended in blood.

Since the bone marrow provides new life to the patient, the nurses told us that May 10 would be her second birthday. The staff all signed a birthday card and posted it on her door.

We were told that the donor's blood type was B positive. Marianela's blood type is O positive, which meant a change of blood type. Weeks after the bone marrow transfusion, the donor's bone marrow would eventually multiply, and Marianela's would diminish. Her blood type would then become B positive. She would also have two sets of DNA. Most of her body would have her original DNA, and her bone marrow and blood would have the donor's DNA.

We were also told that, during this transition period, the donor's WBC remain within the donated tissue and could recognize the recipient as foreign. Therefore, the WBC present in the transplanted tissue could then attack the recipient's body's cells. This is known as graft-versus-host disease (GvHD). The GvHD can produce inflammation in different organs. In our limited understanding of this rather complex issue, we became aware that a patient with GvHD can have problems in the retina, red blotches on the skin, or issues with the intestines.

Despite the potential aftermath of the transplant, Marianela was very aware that Prince Harry was soon to marry Meghan Markle, and my party girl was not going to miss this event. She invited all her daughters and granddaughters to attend the televised ceremony with her. Everyone wore hats, which she said were required. Some were more pleased with the event than others because it was held in the wee morning hours Dallas time. Of course, we were all aware that nothing suppressed her desire to celebrate life.

Speaking of life, Marianela found out the nurse who had originally shaved her head was pregnant. After congratulating her on the new life she was carrying, Marianela wanted to get a gift for her baby. I thought she would want to go shopping once we were home—but no, she had other plans. She remembered the gift shop where Mari asked for directions on the day she was first admitted in December. I tried to reason with her, telling her that the gift shop was in another building. Nothing would change her mind. She told me we were going, got up from her bed, and headed for the door. She had to sign out by writing her name and the time of departure.

There was a peaceful garden on the north side of the cancer center that we often saw from her room window. Instead of going through an enclosed bridge that connected our building to the rest of the complex, she asked to go through the garden. We sat there for some time. She loved the outdoors. Then she began to walk across the street to the next building. I gave her my arm to steady her weak steps, and I pushed her IV pole. Crossing the street meant walking on a steep incline. She was winded after that effort, but we made it to the gift shop.

She looked all through the shop, evaluating the items against the prices. She was always a thrifty shopper, and I knew better than to rush her. She thought there might be another gift shop, perhaps with more baby items, closer to their maternity building. I told her I was very familiar with the entire complex; the maternity building was on the other side, too far to walk.

"I can make it," she said.

We then began our slow walk and would stop to rest. We finally made it to the other gift shop. She once again began looking at items slowly and intently, then she remembered there was an item in the original gift shop that was better and more affordable. I suggested that we go back to her room, through the bridge, so she could get some rest. However, I was actually the one who needed the rest. She wasn't having any of that, so we headed back to the original gift shop. Finally she purchased the baby gift, and we headed back to her room. When we got to the nurses' station, she had to sign back with the time. I realized we had been walking for almost two hours. I was ready to call an Uber toward the end of our hike!

Days later she determined that the pregnant nurse was off duty, but the other nurses said her husband was a nurse on another floor. I took Marianela to the other floor, so she could give him the baby's gift.

After weeks in the hospital, her blood work showed that she was well on her way to recovery, so we were allowed to go home. Daily visits to the doctor showed she was improving. Some visits were two hours. Some were six or eight. Either way, we welcomed them because at the end of each one, we went home. We were constantly reminded to take care to avoid any infections. Constant handwashing, hand sanitizers, and face masks were the order of the day.

During the next few months, we saw Marianela getting better. We were all used to the routine visits, tests, transfusions, and medications. I remembered the doctor saying we would have a new normal. I guess this was part of it. Even though the doctor had said Marianela was going to tire easily and take naps, this was not part of her new normal. She continued to amaze us with her strength and faith.

Dear God, I too have faith in you. On this faith, I stand and ask you to increase it. I believe that I will need more faith to see me through this.

# 15

# THE SETBACK

In early November 2018, Marianela began having stomach issues. We had been instructed to report any changes in her status. We did and were directed to take her to the emergency room, one especially dedicated to transplant patients. They performed tests, and the results indicated that she had a minor intestinal infection. An antibiotic was prescribed, and we went home. Her health improved for a few days.

The following week she began having the same symptoms. Again we followed procedure: report the issue, go to the ER, get more tests, and wait for the results. Again we were told that she had a slight infection. We got a new prescription and went back home. But this time we noticed she was getting weaker each day. The improvement pattern had reversed.

On November 16, 2018, we took her back to the ER, but this time she was admitted into the hospital. After a series of new tests, she was diagnosed with GvHD; the previous infections caused the donor's WBC to fight the infection. This caused her own WBC to see the donor's WBC as foreign, and the battle began. The donor's WBC then began attacking Marianela's cells in her intestine.

She was administered very strong antibiotics and antifungal medicines. As the days passed, she did not improve. In fact, she kept getting weaker. Her intestines could not digest her food, so she was put on an intravenous supplement and fed through an IV.

The almost daily blood and platelet transfusions kept the medical staff very busy. Prior to this, a blood transfusion would keep her HBG numbers up for two or three days; this time they were dropping daily.

During the next few days, she started getting diarrhea. It became so intense that any time she got up from her bed, she hemorrhaged. We all encouraged her to straighten up and take a few steps around the room, but it was apparent that she was just too weak. Gradually she began eating some small milkshakes and ice pops, but it did not last. She eventually rejected them, and we would just throw them away.

We would pray the rosary daily with her, and she would often fall asleep during the prayer. One day, when I was the only one in the room, she asked me to get closer.

When I did, she whispered, "I'm dying."

Her statement stopped me cold. What happened to her enthusiasm, her strength, her willingness to fight through this? I tried to convince her that she was not dying. This was very difficult, as I spoke through my tears. She told me she was ready, and I should just keep taking care of our family. Thank God that no one else was in the room. I had managed to console myself by the time everyone else came back.

> *Fear not death's decree for you; remember, it embraces those before you, and those after.*
> —*Sirach 41:3 (New American Bible Version)*

# 16

## GLORIOUS TRANSITION

Marianela did not decorate our home for Christmas that year because she was in the hospital. I didn't either because I was rarely there. My daughter visited us from San Antonio a few days before the holidays. All three of our daughters decided to decorate, even if it was in a limited fashion. Once they finished, they took pictures and showed them to their mom. She smiled and was grateful. They even put a small Christmas tree in her hospital room.

During her time in the hospital, Marianela always had someone stay with her overnight. Most of the time, it was me. On the weekend, one of our daughters would stay, so I could go home and take care of things. When her sister visited us from Laredo, she would stay with her.

On December 26, 2018, my daughter from San Antonio volunteered to stay with her mom overnight. I went home with the rest of the family that night. The next day, as we got ready to return to the hospital, I received a phone call. My daughter informed me the doctor had just left and told them that the end was near. They had tried every antibiotic and antifungal possible. She had not responded favorably to any of them. There was nothing else they could do. I realized Marianela knew the outcome before the doctors did, recalling the night that she told me she was dying.

Marianela and I had prepared for this moment years earlier. We had purchased a compartment in the columbarium at our parish. We had written our wills. We had executed a medical power of attorney and an advance directive. I brought these two items with me to the hospital and presented them to the doctor as soon as we arrived. They read them and thanked me. They said when patients have these, it takes the burden off of them to make the decision.

When we arrived in her room, we saw Marianela lying in her bed. She appeared to be unconscious. Everyone was very somber. All I could do was stare at her and recall all the moments that we had shared together: the *lunada*, the *quinceañera*, our engagement, our wedding, the birth of our daughters, the birth and passing of our son…and now this. *Was this the last day that we would be together? Would this be our last memory?* All I could do was hold her hand and kiss it.

Around her bed were our daughters, sons-in-law, grandchildren, her sister, brother-in-law, and two nieces. We were all reliving the many moments that we had enjoyed with her. She would always brighten up any room. One of her many doctors came into the room to see if we needed anything. We told him that we were as good as could be expected.

He said, "Look at the room. Look at everyone around her bed. Feel the love that surrounds her. Guess what? She won!"

How true that was. All her life she reflected God's love. *Now she is receiving God's love from her family.*

*Sing a new song to the Lord, who has done marvelous deeds, whose right hand and holy arm have won the victory.*
*—Psalms 98:1 (New American Bible Version)*

A good friend of ours would often say, "I can't wait to see what God is going to do next." I recalled that and said it in her room that afternoon. I looked at the clock and saw that it was 3:00 p.m. I suggested that we pray the "Chaplet of Divine Mercy." We sang it while standing around Marianela's bed. I recalled them singing the "Divine Mercy" around my bed when I was unconscious years earlier.

A lady came into the room as soon as we finished. She had visited Marianela many times during her many stays in the hospital. She sang opera and played the harp. Years ago she used to perform in Italy. Hearing is one of the last senses that a person loses, so her mission was to reach out to those in their last stage of life. The soothing music comforts not only the patient but also the family members. Her harp was very unique. Most harps rest on the right shoulder of the person playing it. She had hers specially made to rest on her left shoulder because she wanted her music to come from her heart. Indeed it did. When I told this lady that we would soon be losing Marianela, she asked if she could sing for her. The first two songs that she played on her harp and sang were "Ave Maria" and "Gentle

Woman." Little did she know that these were the two songs that Marianela had always requested to be played at her funeral. She continued playing and singing for sixty minutes. When she finished, our pastor, Father Tom, walked into the room. He anointed her and forgave all her sins, and, ten minutes later, Marianela left us. We were all able to witness the peace of our Lord at that moment.

The last words that Nelly spoke were, "Thank you, Jesus."

Yes, thank you, Jesus, for having given me a beautiful life called Marianela. It seems that now I understood my hallucination and how those children felt having an empty hole instead of a heart. My heart had just been taken from me.

Now I have seen my beautiful girl take her next step. She has been an amazing example of God's love to our family and friends throughout her life on this earth.

Until we meet again, babe.

# 17

## LOVE LETTERS

My dearest Marianela,

It seems like just yesterday that I first saw you under the light of the moon. I can still see your eyes close slightly as you smiled. You were wearing white Bermuda shorts and a blouse with pineapples on it. I can still hear all our friends talking, laughing, and singing. I remember that Esperanza was the one who took you to the *lunada*. I am forever grateful to her for having done that.

That night my heart filled with hope, hope that we would share our lives together. I was also filled with doubt that you didn't know who I was or would not have the same interest in me that I had in you. Now you know that it was because of my shyness that I didn't talk to you.

When I called you a few days later, and you began speaking to me on the phone, you sounded so sweet. Every time I called you, I kept looking for some sign that you liked me too. You were so much fun to talk to.

It was easy to converse even through my shyness. You made me feel so at ease.

I can't tell you how happy you made me when you said you would go with me to the festival in October. I was so nervous as the festival got closer. I hoped that I wouldn't make a fool of myself that night and that there would be other dates.

To my surprise, there *were* other dates. I am so glad for those dates because they led to our lives together.

The happiest day of my life was when we were married. I still wondered if it was just a dream. But this real event led to other dreams that, together, we made real. The most important dreams that came true were our three daughters and a son. How blessed we are to have them be a part of our lives. Our six grandchildren are also very special blessings that our Lord gave us. And you, with your faith-filled heart, raised them and guided them through their childhood.

I can never thank you enough for always being by my side. Whenever I was told I had to relocate to another city, you would always say yes. Whatever we were going through, you would always be there. Your constant support, constant faith, and constant love never failed. You always carried us in the good times and in the not-so-good times.

When we lost our son, I noticed you felt hurt by God. You pulled back from him, as did I. But as usual, you thought more of others, of our daughters, than of yourself. You fought the disappointment with God for the sake of our family. You still showed our girls how important God is in our lives. I always knew that we would get past the loss of our son, and we did.

When I got sick, and they told you that I was very sick and would not make it, you stayed by my side, as did our family and friends. You never gave up hope. You never stopped praying. You always kept believing in God to see me through, and he did.

When I kept hearing how sick I was and that my organs were failing, I didn't give up. I didn't want to die just yet. I knew we all would die sometime, but I didn't want to die before you. I didn't want to leave you alone. Although you wouldn't have been alone, not with our family around you. I wanted to be there for you when your time came. I wanted to hold your hand and kiss you goodbye one last time. And thanks to God, I did.

Seeing you as you went through all your illness was so difficult for me, but it was very rewarding. I got to see you live your life to the fullest, and I got to see you pass the same way. You always reflected God's love to everyone, every day. I still have total strangers tell me how much you meant to them and how you, to this day, affect their lives.

I now ask you to forgive me for whatever I did that was wrong in our lives. I'm sorry that we didn't get to visit Ireland, but I'm certain we will eventually. I'm sorry you weren't able to hold your son. I can only imagine how much that hurt you. Now I just ask you to keep praying for me and for our family. Please continue to look out for us and protect us. I ask you to be with me when my time comes, so that I can also take that last step on this earth with the love and faith that you did.

As Monsignor O'Gorman said in your one-year anniversary Mass in San Antonio, "If given the choice for her to come back to us or to stay where she is, I guarantee you that she would not come back." And I don't blame you. Why would you?

Remember that I used to write you poems when we were dating? I found this one that is appropriate at this time, although I wrote it in July 1963.

## Whenever You're Away

The sun does not show its face
Whenever you're away,
And if it does, I cannot tell
Because I feel so gray.
Your friendly voice, your lovely face
I do not see or hear,
Nor all the joys which I do feel
Whenever you are near.
I miss you often telling me,
"I truly love you so."
For when I heard it last was when
You said that you must go.
When you're away I cannot help
But pray for your return,
Because, my love, your being near
I truly often yearn.
When you're away I realize

How much you mean to me
And feel secure our love will last
For all eternity.

I look forward to the day when we will once again be together in paradise.

Love always,
David

■ ■ ■

My dearest children,
Please know how proud I am of each one of you. You have all grown to be beautiful in the sight of God and in the sight of Lita and me. There hasn't been a single day that I don't think about you and pray for you. Never forget how much Lita and I love you.

She and I were so grateful for you being around her bed as she said farewell to us. It made it much easier and more memorable for both of us. She will continue to look after us, as she always did, and will continue to love us and hold us in her arms.

Lita always had so much faith in our Lord and continually passed it on to you. She was a true witness of our total belief in God. I trust that you too will always be a witness to those around you. To go on a pilgrimage is to walk toward God while taking others with you. While our pilgrimage continues, Lita's has ended. She is no longer walking toward God; she is with him already. But know that she is still taking others to God.

I know how much each of you love Lita and how much you love me. When Lita and I began dating, we had many dreams. You are those dreams from years ago. I ask God's blessings upon you as you make your dreams come true.

As you have seen, life has its good times and not-so-good times. But also, as you have seen, God is always with us. His loving arms are always there to support us and to help us up when we fall. We must be aware of his presence in our lives. Look for those miracles because they are there. Thank him for them and let others know about them.

A friend of mine would say, "We are not bodies with a soul. We are souls with a body." This helps us to cope in times of grief because we can realize that dying is simply a shedding of our body while continuing to exist.

As Mari said, "When we die, we have not left. We have simply shed our cocoon and are now flying freely." Be aware and enjoy it as Lita flies around you daily.

God bless you.

Love always,
Papa David

■ ■ ■

My dear Heavenly Father,

You truly are an amazing planner. I am astounded as to how well you coordinate things, things like the planets in our universe, the fish in the water, and the birds in the air. I know you also had a hand in making the *lunada* happen, in taking Marianela and me there so that we would meet. That was the start of something big, our lives and our family.

All the days of our lives, every minute, you watched over us and kept us in your care. Every day, whether it was bad or glad, you were there for us. Even if we didn't understand the why, you were there to see us through it all. We always felt your presence and your love. Your care for all your children is sometimes questioned, but in the end, we realize that it's been there all along.

You saw your son die as I saw mine. You must have wept as he said, "Into your hand I commend my spirit." I also wept when I saw my son die. But this unbelievable pain was, in the end, worth it. Jesus's death meant redemption for all humanity. I thank you for that. When my son died, it meant that now we have an angel in heaven looking out for us.

Now that Marianela has passed, we have another angel in heaven also looking out for each of us.

As much as I miss her, I am glad that she is with you, where she is meant to be. There is no other place that I want her to be. She dedicated all her life to you.

And now I know that you have her in your kingdom.
Thank you, dear Lord.
    Remember me always.

Your faithful servant,
David

# 18

# THE PRESENT

"Every cloud has a silver lining." This is so true, especially if you believe in and trust God.

Now that I have had the opportunity to reflect on my life, I see the beauty of it all. God has truly given us all such a present. His marvelous gift to us cannot be explained. Even when we experience difficult moments in our lives, we see the silver lining. I'm not saying that we don't experience pain. I'm saying that if you have God in your life, he will see you through it.

I saw the growth in my daughters' faith as a result of their brother's passing. Although they were very young when this occurred, they relied on our Lord to heal their pain. Unfortunately, Marianela and I were not there for them as we should have been given that we were dealing with his passing as well. As rain waters the flowers, our tears made the love in our hearts grow. This event increased the faith in each of us.

My health issue in 2015 stressed family and friends. And since I was able to hear everything that was happening, I was stressed as well. But it was this stress that led to so many prayers that turned the situation around. It was also my ability to be aware of how critical I was that helped me to use my mind to begin the healing process. This same uneasy time made it possible for all of us to witness God's miracle. These days made us aware of how much we value each other and brought us closer as a family. They also united our many friends to us. To this day, I still have some of them relay their feelings when they visited me in the ICU.

The most impactful event that we have gone through was Marianela's passing. For an entire year, we cared for her. We kept track of her meds, her appointments, her medical files, her test results, etc. We took turns to ensure that she was never alone, either at home or in the hospital. We had to constantly wash our hands, use hand sanitizer, wear masks because her defenses were very low. Little did we know that we were being prepared for dealing with COVID-19.

Often, my daughters and I reflect that it would be very difficult for Marianela to deal with this quarantine. She would be in a very vulnerable situation due to her autoimmune deficiency. We all agree that we are glad that she did not have to deal with this situation.

My two oldest granddaughters, Analiese and Roxanne (Sanny), graduated from college and are each working using their degrees in psychology. Their sister, Lauren, also graduated from college with a degree in community health. She was so very impressed and grateful with the care that was given to her grandmother by the nurses that she decided to return to college to get a degree in nursing. She will graduate in December 2020.

My grandson, David, is in college. His sisters, Kaylie and Meredith, are in high school and middle school, respectively. They often talk about the time they had with their grandmother. Marianela had such a gift that she could relate to anyone regardless of age.

My daughters frequently talk. They have always been very close to each other. But now it seems that they are even closer. They realize that Marianela wanted them to be there for each other and for me. They are always tending after me. Anjanette prepares meals for me on the weekend, so all I have to do is put them in the microwave. Roxanne often has us over to her house to enjoy some feast, whether it's a grilled steak or a seafood boil prepared by Nathan. Mari has immerged herself more into her painting. She is the one who painted the front cover of this book. When she and Raul visit from San Antonio, he always tends to matters needing attention around the house. I am so blessed by having my family and friends.

Marianela's sister, the one who used to accompany us on our dates to the movies, reaches out to us daily. She and her family constantly reflect their love and concern for us. Marianela would be so proud of each of us and how we are bonding even more now that she has passed. I can see her approving smile.

Now I am aware that the empty hole, the space where my heart used to be, is now completely full. The hearts of my friends, of my family, of my Marianela, and above all, of my God now reside there.

Now that we are all in quarantine, we all had to decide how we spend it. I have always told my family that time will pass, whether we do anything with it or not. I began writing this book shortly after I got out of the hospital in 2015. For some reason, I didn't follow through. I was convinced that I was not a writer and would never be able to write a book. Now that I was faced with the quarantine, I decided that God was giving me the time to complete this task. I prayed and told God that if he saw fit to give me the time, he should also give me the words, and he did. He has performed yet another miracle.

Thank you once again, God.

Do you realize that you are holding one of God's miracles in your hands? Let me leave you, the reader, with this challenge. List your own miracles that God has given you. I believe that you will be pleasantly surprised. Good luck, and may God bless you.

# EPILOGUE

Reflecting on my life, I am aware of its ups and downs. We all have them. But somehow the downs seem to have faded away and given way to the ups. We must have the lows so that we can enjoy the highs.

The fifth joyful mystery is the finding of our Lord in the temple. That would not have been possible unless Mary and Joseph experienced his loss. We would not have the basis of our faith, the resurrection of Jesus, without his death on the cross.

Marianela and I would not have an angel in heaven without the experience of our son's death. This also applies to our daughters who suffered the pain of having their brother pass. But now they also have an angel in heaven caring for them.

I had an ordeal that almost took my life. It inflicted much pain on Marianela and our daughters, sons-in-law, and grandchildren. It also impacted our friends. But the pain brought us all together in prayer and strengthened our faith. It also gave me a glimpse of the afterlife. It was because I came so close to death that I was given the opportunity to live more fully, to be there for my lady. This has also allowed me to share my experience with others. But most of all, it has given me the honor of glorifying my Lord.

A close friend of our family lost her father. The funeral Mass was very well attended. Before the Mass began, I saw my friend and asked her to notice how many were in attendance. She was very grateful to see all her father's friends. I could then assure her that there were many more friends receiving him into heaven.

After the many weeks of recovery, I did not know why I was still on this earth. What else did God need me to do? Years later it all became clear. As Marianela had been there for me through my rough times, God permitted me to be there for her during her difficult journey. We had always been there for each other, and this was no exception.

I am so thankful for the opportunity to help her through this. How blessed I have been to be able to take her to doctor's appointments, to keep track of her medications, to be with her during hospital stays, to accompany her on the walk to purchase that perfect baby gift for her nurse.

But most of all, I have been blessed by being able to open doors for her. When we began dating, I wanted to make a good impression, so I would be as courteous as possible. I would walk on the curbside of the sidewalk. Should there ever be a car that would jump the curb, I would be ready to protect her. I don't know what my 160-pound body would do against a vehicle, but the intention was good.

The other thing that I would always do is open the door for her, whether it was her front door, a door to a building, or the car door. Several years later my reasons for doing these things changed. I no longer needed to make a good impression, but I did want to show my appreciation to her. I felt that this was the least I could do in return for her sharing her life with me. I opened the door to the car up until I took her to the hospital for that last time.

On the last day that she was with us, as she lay in her hospital bed, I once again opened a door for her. I leaned over and softly told her it was OK to take her next step. I assured her that we would be fine, thanked her for the many years that we had been together, and gave her a kiss. As she finally took her last step, I am certain that the door to heaven was opened for her by another David. At last, she was able to see her son and embrace him.

> *When Jesus saw his mother and the disciple there whom he loved, he said to his mother, "Woman, behold your son." Then he said to his disciple, "Behold your mother."*
> *—John 19:26–27 (New American Bible Version)*

Sweetheart, I have absolutely no doubt that you are with God. May God bless you and hold you forever, babe. I will always love you.

> *Let all on earth worship and sing praise to you, sing praise to your name! Come and see the works of God, awesome in the deeds done for us.*
> *—Psalms 66:4–5 (New American Bible Version)*

Some months later I read a book entitled *The Prophet* by Kahlil Gibran. One line stood out from the chapter on death. It said, "And when the earth shall claim your limbs, then shall you truly dance." I recalled all the dances Marianela and I went to. She was an excellent dancer. I believe that now she is truly dancing in heaven.

Dear God, I thank you for all the blessings that you have bestowed on us, especially that amazing one called Marianela. I thank you for my family, friends, and support group. I ask that you continue to bless us with your Holy Spirit that fills us with your love and peace so that we can continue to do your holy will.

May we all forever glorify you and thank you for our everlasting love. Please take care of us all…and take care of my little girl. Amen.

*Now that I am old and gray, do not forsake me, God, that I may proclaim your might to all generations yet to come, your power and justice, God, to the highest heaven. You have done great things; O God, who is your equal?*
*—Psalms 71:18 (New American Bible Version)*

*With an everlasting love,*

*Marianela and David*

Connect with him on Facebook at: www.facebook.com/
lovespeaksbook. To connect with his daughter, Mari who
painted the front cover go to www.facebook.com/1artsymari.

Made in the USA
Columbia, SC
22 October 2020

23289788R00088